BE A TEAMMATE WI
YOURSELF
Understanding Trauma and Dissociation

Hong Wang Fung
Colin A. Ross, M.D.

Manitou Communications, Inc.

1701 Gateway, Suite 349
Richardson, TX 75080
Phone: 972-918-9588

www.manitoucommunications.com
www.rossinst.com
rossinst@rossinst.com

ISBN: 978-1-7321000-6-0

Library of Congress Catalog Number: 2019936593

Hong Wang Fung, Colin A. Ross

Be A Teammate With Yourself: Understanding Trauma and Dissociation

1. Dissociation 2. Trauma 3. Self-Help

Description

This is a psychoeducation book designed for people who suffer from mental health problems after traumatic or stressful experiences. Persons who have a trauma-related mental disorder (e.g., post-traumatic stress disorder, borderline personality disorder, dissociative disorder) may also benefit from this self-help resource. This book will not and cannot replace any clinical assessment or treatment. It aims to enable readers to understand post-traumatic and dissociative reactions, learn heathy coping strategies and remain hopeful for recovery.

Author Bios

Hong Wang Fung is a social worker and a researcher from Hong Kong. He is the founder of the Hong Kong Association Concerning Dissociative Disorders (HKACDD). His research focuses on trauma-related mental disorders, pathological dissociation and social work practice. Email: andyhwfung@gmail.com.

Colin A. Ross is a psychiatrist from North America and is an internationally renowned expert in the field of trauma and dissociation. He is a past President of the International Society for the Study of Trauma and Dissociation (ISSTD) (1993–1994) as well as the founder and President of The Colin A. Ross Institute for Psychological Trauma. Website: www.rossinst.com. Email: rossinst@rossinst.com. Dr. Ross is a co-founder of Trauma Education Essentials (www.traumaedessentials.com) with his daughter, Dr. Dana Ross, who is a psychiatrist in Toronto.

Disclaimer

The contents of this book are provided for information purposes only. None of the information is medical advice. The information is not intended to provide a clinical assessment nor take the place of proper medical advice from a qualified medical practitioner. You access and use the information at your own risk.

TABLE OF CONTENTS

Chapter 1: Introduction – How To Use This Book

This chapter aims to:

1) Enable readers to have reasonable expectations for this book
2) Discuss common challenges for persons who have trauma and dissociation

This is an educational book designed for people who have mental health problems after a single or multiple traumatic or stressful experiences. Examples of these experiences include, but are not limited to: disaster, serious accident, war, disease or injury, medical procedure, peer bullying, family violence, physical abuse, emotional abuse, sexual abuse, physical neglect, emotional neglect and other extreme events (e.g., homicide, suicide, death of a close friend or relative), no matter whether they occur during childhood or adulthood.

Scientific findings reveal that trauma and stress are associated with many physical and mental health problems. In particular, it is common and understandable for survivors to develop post-traumatic and dissociative reactions, which could lead to serious distress and disability. Examples of post-traumatic and dissociative reactions include: re-experiencing the painful memories, emotional numbness, avoiding things related to the trauma, being emotionally unstable, sleep problems, memory problems, difficulties in relationships, somatic symptoms, identity dissociation, etc.

If the post-traumatic and dissociative reactions remain unrelieved, some survivors may partially or fully meet the diagnostic criteria for certain mental disorders, such as post-traumatic stress disorder (PTSD), borderline personality disorder (BPD) and/or a dissociative disorder. It is also not rare for survivors to have other mental health problems, such as depression, anxiety, eating disorders and psychotic symptoms.

Some people may feel okay after experiencing a traumatic or stressful event, but trauma and stress could also lead to serious mental health problems in some people. Perhaps you had some difficult experiences in the past, and you are probably still facing a lot of challenges now. You should know that it is already a very good start for you to seek help – you are reading this book, which means that your recovery journey has already started!!

It is important to note that recovery is always possible. Many mental health problems after trauma and stress are understandable – they usually have survival and self-defense purposes. Although it takes time and effort, many survivors can reduce their symptoms considerably and recover very well. Successfully recovered cases have been reported in many clinical studies and books.

So, what is the content of this book? This book is specifically written for people who have experienced trauma or stress, and for people with any kind of post-traumatic and dissociative reactions. This book discusses the impacts of trauma and stress on our body and mind and the common post-traumatic and dissociative reactions. This book also talks about the challenges and life problems that survivors often encounter. Moreover, it introduces some practical self-help methods. Hopefully, readers would find this book easy-to-read and useful.

In addition, this book introduces some practical self-help skills; readers need to practice and work on the exercises after each chapter and in daily life in order to master the skills and maximize the effects of this book.

While this book is written based on the clinical wisdom and scientific findings from the trauma and dissociation literature, this book will not, should not and cannot replace any conventional treatment or service (including but not limited to medical treatment, psychotherapy, counselling and other social services). Conventional care service is usually important for many people with mental health problems. This book is only an additional resource that readers may benefit from. In case of emergency and crisis situations, you need to seek help immediately in your community (e.g., call the police, go to your nearest emergency service).

There are 12 chapters in total. Each chapter will have a different focus. Please be patient, and go slowly – read this book little by little, paragraph by paragraph. You can always review the content you find relevant, and practice the exercises you find helpful. There is no quick fix for recovery – but recovery is always achievable.

Oh, by the way, 'be a teammate with yourself' is the main theme of the entire book. Do you know why?

Trauma and stress often make us have conflicts with ourselves (e.g., having feelings that we don't want to have, crying, shaking or yelling out when we don't want to do so, living with an angry child inside us). To recover from trauma and stress, from this perspective, is to acknowledge, accept and integrate our bio-psycho-social experiences and be a good teammate with our body and mind. Remember, we should not and can never eliminate any parts of ourselves, even if they do not seem like they belong to us.

You basically have a common goal with your body and mind. Although conflicts may occur among different parts of you in the beginning, you all want to survive and you all want to have pleasure and avoid pain in nature. Being a good teammate with yourself is one important thing you need to do in your recovery journey. We will discuss this further later in the book.

So, are you ready to start your journey?

Remember, go slow!

All the best!!!

Assignment 1.1

What changes do you expect to occur as a result of your efforts in reading this book? Please try to write down a few things that you think would possibly get better in your life after completing the journey of these 12 chapters.

Assignment 1.2

Everyone needs help sometimes in life, but seeking help could be a difficult step. What makes you want to read this book and improve your life?

Question 1: Does the content in this chapter relate to your experience?
1 = Strongly disagree; 10 = Strongly agree

Question 2: Have you learned this content before?
1 = Strongly disagree; 10 = Strongly agree

Chapter 2: Safety Is The Primary Consideration

This chapter aims to:

1) Discuss the common challenges in life and suggest some possible solutions

2) Assist readers to devise their own crisis plans and remain safe

Safety is the primary issue in the journey of recovery. It is very difficult for a person in danger to manage his/her negative experiences (e.g., anxiety, sadness, panic, helplessness, anger), let alone cope with the symptoms. Ongoing trauma and chronic stress could make the symptoms worse. Therefore, in case you live in a traumatic or stressful environment that is obviously influencing you, it is important for you to consider changing the situation or staying away from it.

If you live with a person who repeatedly abuses or hurts you, no matter whether it is physically or emotionally, you need to think about whether you can stop his/her harmful behaviors or you should stay away from him/her.

For a little child, since self-protection is not possible, it is necessary for a child to depend on other people (e.g., parents or caretakers). This makes a child easily hurt. While you can't control or prevent what happened in the past, when you grow up, you become more able to protect yourself.

It is not easy to change your living situation. It can be a very difficult decision. You may have many considerations to work through. For example, you may think that he/she does not have the intention to hurt you, or that he/she only has some misunderstanding or bad habits. Or, you may not want a relationship breakup because he/she is one of the important persons in your life. Also, what comes to your mind may be: are you financially independent enough to leave the one who hurts you? Can you live without having his/her support? It is totally understandable to have many concerns and worries. However, if you still live in a traumatic or stressful environment, your mood may continue to be affected.

You may want to discuss your situation with someone who you can trust, or you can seek help from helping professionals (e.g., social workers, psychologists, medical doctors). You can at least hear what they have to say. They may also provide you with some resources. If there are financial or housing problems that affect your decision, they may also give you some advice. Helping professionals should be more familiar with the local community resources that you may find helpful. In case of immediate risk (e.g., family violence, child abuse), you should also find helping professionals and/or emergency service providers to ensure your own safety and the safety of vulnerable family members at home (e.g., children).

Having care and support from family, partners and friends is very important for recovery. If you have support from others, you can discuss your problems with them, and seek help from them, physically or spiritually. For some survivors, however, it may be difficult to have enough care and support from others. We should be grateful when we have someone who is willing to support us. Sometimes your family members or friends may misunderstand your mental health problems, or they may have done something that hurt you. This could be very upsetting for you, but you need to know that not everyone is familiar with mental health and psychology and has enough knowledge. Of course, if this leads to a lot of traumatic and stressful experiences, you need to consider changing the situation or staying away from it, as mentioned above. Otherwise, you may want to have a sincere communication with the persons involved, acknowledge their support, tell them your feelings, and provide some accurate information for them, if possible and if they want it. If this is not very possible, you may need to think about how to avoid conflicts and stress.

In some regions (e.g., some Asian countries), studying may be very stressful, especially if you have mental health problems. Prolonged stressful experience (e.g., public examinations, too much homework) could make it hard for you to focus on the journey of recovery. Your symptoms may also affect your study. Thus, sometimes it is necessary to consider if it is better to stop your study for a while in order to focus on recovery. You may need to discuss this with your therapist if that is possible.

Some people with mental health problems are capable of working. Yet, it also makes sense if you feel it is difficult to work. Sometimes, work can be very stressful and may even trigger your emotions. A stressful job or a duty that triggers your emotions may also make it hard to focus on the journey of recovery. If your duty involves high risks (e.g., aircraft pilot, police, firefighter) or working with vulnerable groups (e.g., children, persons with mental retardation), you especially need to seek help early. If you have financial problems, social welfare organizations and community resources may help too. It is totally fine to seek help from other people and/or from social welfare organizations when you need to do so. You can return to work after dealing with your mental health problems. You are just out of commission for the time being.

Crisis planning is an important part of recovery

You can use positive and constructive behavioral repertoires to remain safe. As you learn and practice these coping strategies, it becomes easier to let go of your old unhealthy ways of coping. Just like learning to ride a bike, play the piano, or any other skill, practice is essential. The first step in crisis planning is to review the past and make a list of the kinds of crises you have experienced. What are the triggers? How did you react to them? Could any of these situations have been predicted or avoided? You can make a mental list of your crises, or, even better a written list that you can review. Sometimes sticky notes or flash cards can be useful, or you can keep lists in your phone.

Once you have a list or inventory of past crises, then you can add to it by listing positive coping strategies for each of them. Don't wait for a crisis to happen. Plan ahead. Practice your new coping skills when there is only a small crisis, or no crisis at all. You can use the grounding skills and the internal communication skills described elsewhere in this book, and you can make up strategies of your own. Whatever works for you is good. Sometimes just taking a break from life and allowing yourself a little down time can be helpful. A bath, a walk, reading a book, watching TV, anything that de-escalates your mind and body can help to make a crisis seem smaller and less of a catastrophe.

You also need to work on your self-talk as part of your crisis planning, including how you talk to your internal team members. Are you being a calm, safe adult for them, or are you making them feel more scared and unprotected by how you react? In cognitive therapy, there is an error of thinking called *catastrophization*. This occurs when you make a crisis seem much bigger than it is, and tell yourself it is a bigger disaster than it actually is in the present. This can happen because you are getting triggered into the past again. You can remind yourself that this is the present, not the past; you are bigger now and have supports, skills and resources you didn't have as a child.

Assignment 2.1

Do you think you can prepare your own crisis plan so that you can follow it in case of need? Your crisis plan may include: possible coping strategies; available support in your network; available community services; practical needs (e.g., do you need someone to look after your children); and contacts for local emergency services. Please try to write your answers down. You may want to discuss your plan with your social worker, therapist or doctor too.

Assignment 2.2

Chronic stress and ongoing trauma can significantly affect your mental health. Can you recognize some of the sources of stress in your daily life? Do you think it is necessary to consider staying away from some of the stressors?

Question 1: Does the content in this chapter relate to your experience?
1 = Strongly disagree; 10 = Strongly agree

Question 2: Have you learned this content before?
1 = Strongly disagree; 10 = Strongly agree

Chapter 3: Basic Self-Help Skills

This chapter aims to:

1) Introduce some basic self-help skills
2) Enable readers to better manage their symptoms
3) Help readers better prepare for future challenges

As mentioned in the first chapter, it is important to be patient to deal with trauma and recover from the mental health problems it causes. It is not safe to go through the traumatic or painful memories too early. Don't force yourself to solve your problems and get well too quickly. Your symptoms and experiences may sometimes make you feel pain, or affect your life in different aspects (e.g., social life, work, study, sleep, emotions, behaviors). Thus, in the beginning of your recovery journey, there are some skills that you need to learn and practice. Imagine you are going to start a new journey; you need to have good equipment and prepare for any challenge before you start. This book gives you some guides for the journey, and the following skills and advice can be your good equipment.

1. Grounding

There may be times that you feel unreal, anxious, nervous or frightened even when there is nothing to threaten you. For example, some people may suddenly feel very nervous and start sweating and trembling even though they are in a safe place (e.g., office, school, restaurant, bus). Some people may have flashbacks of traumatic memories – the memories could be very vivid and terrifying to the point that the painful event in the past seems to be happening again in the present moment.

When such symptoms occur, it is not likely that you are living in the present moment – you are re-living the past when the trauma happened, and your body is repeating the physiological response (e.g., rapid heartbeat, sweating, increased adrenaline) which had been activated during a painful experience.

To deal with this kind of symptom, you need to bring yourself back to the present moment – a safe place. Grounding techniques can be used for this purpose.

There are several ways to do so:

- Tell yourself that you are safe now by describing your surroundings, for example: "Now, it is already September, 2019, I am 30 years old. I now am in my room, it is 9 PM. No one can hurt me now. I am safe, and I am capable of protecting myself."

- Name 3 things you can see, and then name 3 things you can hear, and then name 3 things you can feel – do it slowly.
- Drink some warm water – taste it very slowly. Notice your feelings mindfully.
- Shuffle your feet on the floor, squeeze your fists, look around, stand up.

Grounding is basically a strategy for you to connect yourself with the present moment. In other words, by doing this, you can shift your attention away from the distress and focus on the here and now. This could help you calm yourself down and cope with anxiety, panic and flashbacks.

2. Breathing

Sometimes you want to sleep but you just can't. Sometimes you want to relax but you may feel very tense. It is probably because your body is alert as if there is a predator hunting you, or as if you are in danger.

There are many systems inside your body. When your body identifies any potential or actual danger (e.g., a fire, a tiger, an angry parent, a very rapid car), the sympathetic nervous system (SNS) will become very active so that you can be ready to respond to the danger (e.g., fight, flight) in order to survive. It is a very normal animal function. It becomes a problem only if it is overactive even when you want to relax or when the danger is too far away.

In order to make the SNS less active, you could try to activate the parasympathetic nervous system (PSNS), which is responsible for conserving energy (rest and digestion). The SNS and the PSNS function in opposition to each other.

So, how to activate the PSNS then?

Regulating your breathing is a key method to activate your PSNS. Breathing very very deeply, very very slowly – this is a simple but very crucial way to relax everyone's bodies.

3. Coping with triggers

Triggers are the things that stimulate you to have negative emotions, flashbacks of painful memories or other symptoms.

Different people can have different triggers. Almost everything (e.g., a car, a place, a tree, a book, a picture, a word, a conversation, a relationship, a stressful environment) can be a trigger. It is very personal.

You may want to try to identify your own triggers, so that you can better prepare yourself. Try to think of what triggered your emotions or symptoms before.

Some triggers that are harmful should definitely be avoided, such as an abuser or a violent person.

If some triggers cannot be avoided (e.g., your internal feelings or memories), you may use grounding or breathing techniques to cope with those triggers.

If you know you are going to a place where there are certain triggers, you may try to ask a supportive friend to go with you, or you may talk to your social worker or therapist before you go to there. Such crisis planning may be helpful too.

4. Relaxation exercises

Relaxation exercises are helpful for many people. There is research support for them. Apart from the methods we have discussed, there are some other relaxation exercises.

- Body scan: This is a very simple but effective way to relax yourself. To do so, you mentally scan your body, from your head to your foot very slowly – focus on and concentrate on each small part step by step. You need to be mindful and focused – notice the feelings in each part of your body. No need to change anything – accept everything as it is.

- Progressive muscle relaxation exercise: You find a comfortable environment and then relax your body step by step, part by part. For example, you may first pay attention to your forehead, tense the muscles a bit, and then release the tension slowly and slowly – try to 'feel' the difference between tension and relaxation. You could do this repeatedly – after your forehead, try your face, chin, shoulders, hands, back and legs and so on.

Some people may also find mindfulness, yoga, tai chi and sports very helpful. In addition, listening to music is often beneficial. These activities and exercises may all help you relax yourself.

5. Imagery-based techniques

Imagery-based techniques can be very powerful for some people.

For instance, when you are having a very strong but negative emotion, try to visualize this in your internal world – is it like a black ball or a red box or something else? What would you like to do with this? Throw it away? Give it a hug? Or pick it up? Lock it away for a while?

There are times you may hardly feel safe in the real world. Imagery relaxation may be helpful for you. To do so, find a relaxing, quiet and safe place, sit down or lie down comfortably, close your eyes, and then imagine that you are in a very beautiful and peaceful place (e.g., a sandy beach, lakeside or grasslands). Try to imagine and experience what you would see, hear, feel and do in such a nice and relaxing place.

Imagery techniques may or may not work for you. It should be noted that these techniques may make you feel a bit relaxed or comfortable, but could not actually solve the problem. For example, you may be able to use imagery techniques to temporarily control an emotion when you are in the workplace, but you may still need to deal with the unaddressed emotions in the future. Also, please try to be gentle even in your inner world. In case you notice you have some inner teammates or inner members, you need to respect them.

6. **Expressing your emotions in a safe way**

It is okay to feel sad, it is okay to have fear, it is also okay to be angry. Some people have been taught to suppress their emotions since they were just little kids, but it is in fact very natural to have emotions. Emotion comes with reasons, or purposes (e.g., anger could help you generate energy; fear could protect you from danger). Of course, a person could be in trouble if he/she expresses his/her emotions inappropriately in an inappropriate situation. Therefore, in order to prevent emotions being out of control in inappropriate situations, you need to know how to express your emotions in a safe way. Here are some methods for your reference:

- Sports: Sports are a socially acceptable and healthy way to express your emotions and use your excessive energy. When you are really angry or irritated, you may consider playing ball games, swimming, running, or other sports or physical activities.

- Art: Some people really like expressing their emotions through art work (e.g., drawing, writing, playing music). If you have not tried this before, you should give yourself a chance to try!

- Games: Some games such as Whack-A-Mole could be helpful when you have too much emotion as well.

- Talking it out: This may be one of the best ways to express your emotions. Talk to a counsellor, a good friend or someone who is reliable and ready to listen to you. This is not about abreaction or reliving the trauma – just speak it out in a controllable manner. If the emotions become too overwhelming or uncontrollable, calm yourself down using other methods (e.g., grounding techniques) first. Please note that not all people are ready to listen to someone who has a lot of emotions – so, find someone who is mentally ready and willing to listen.

- Hospitalization: This may not be the best choice, but hospitals or other care centers could provide a safe place for you to handle your emotions if they are too overwhelming or uncontrollable to the point that they put you in danger (e.g., if you are very depressed and suicidal).

In addition to expressing your emotions, you may also consider regulating your emotions by doing something that leads to positive emotions (e.g., watch a funny movie, play with your pet, have a good meal). This could be very helpful too.

7. **Delaying the maladaptive behaviors**

Conflicts within the mind are common. You may have certain behaviors that you do not want to do or you know you should not do, such as self-harming behaviors or compulsive repetitive behaviors. It can be upsetting if you cannot stop yourself from doing so.

One possible coping strategy that people find helpful is trying to delay the inappropriate behaviors. Tell yourself that you can resist for 5 minutes, then another 5 minutes, and then another 5 minutes, and so on. The urge for the behavior should disappear as you find you have the power to make this decision to delay it.

8. **Alternative strategies**

Maladaptive behaviors (e.g., compulsive thoughts, over-eating, risk-taking behaviors, self-harm) are strategies that the mind uses to cope with certain problems (e.g., stress, pain, guilt), although they are not healthy coping strategies. It can be very helpful if you can plan some healthier alternative strategies for yourself. Here are some examples:

- If you want to self-harm, you may try to rub some ice over your hand.
- If you are very angry, you may try to rip up some pieces of paper or hit a punching bag or pillow.
- You may also try to replace the maladaptive behaviors by doing something that you enjoy, such as playing video games, watching a funny cartoon that you like, having a nice meal, or hanging out with a good friend.

Try to think of the meanings behind your maladaptive behaviors, and then suggest some healthier alternatives for yourself.

9. **Preparing a distraction box**

Some people find it helpful to prepare a small box for themselves. You may also want to make one for yourself.

This box may include things that make you happy or relaxed (e.g., a photo, a music player, a lovely doll, a cheerful letter), and things that require you to concentrate on them (e.g., a coloring book).

See if this can become part of your 'mental first-aid kit' which can help you manage your symptoms in case of need.

Assignment 3.1

Could you create a list of harmless alternative strategies that you will consider using in the future?

Assignment 3.2

This chapter introduces some strategies for you to manage your symptoms and remain safe. You may also have successfully handled your difficulties using other healthy strategies in the past. Please try to write down what strategies are helpful to you and describe why/how they work.

Question 1: Does the content in this chapter relate to your experience?
1 = Strongly disagree; 10 = Strongly agree

Question 2: Have you learned this content before?
1 = Strongly disagree; 10 = Strongly agree

Chapter 4: Trauma Affects Us In Many Ways, But Is Reversible

This chapter aims to:

1. Discuss the impacts of trauma so as to normalize post-traumatic and dissociative reactions
2. Introduce the concept of dissociation
3. Explain why we should be hopeful of recovery

To a certain degree, trauma is very subjective. An event could be traumatic for someone but not for others. Generally speaking, trauma occurs when an event overwhelms one's ability to process and integrate the experience.

While certain major events such as serious accidents, sexual abuse, war and natural disasters are often traumatic, many other adversities could result in traumatization too. For example, it is not rare for people to be traumatized after emotional abuse, emotional neglect, peer bullying, death of a loved one, medical procedures, interpersonal problems, family violence or other unpleasant experiences.

During and after a traumatic event, a person may feel frightened and helpless, may not know how to respond to the event, may have a sense of powerlessness, or may feel like his/her body is out of control. It is also possible for him/her to feel very numb, have no emotions, and behave as if everything is normal. Some people have problems immediately after the traumatic event, and some people start to have problems later (after days, months or even years).

The impacts of trauma on a person can be profound, and multiple. Trauma could affect a person in terms of the cognitive, behavioral, emotional, interpersonal and even physiological aspects of self. Why?

Trauma may make a person feel like the world is dangerous and unpredictable.

Trauma may make a person think that no one can be trusted.

Trauma may make a person believe that he/she is not loveable.

Trauma may make a person feel very angry, depressed or frightened.

Trauma may make a person try hard to avoid any similar situations and anything that could remind him/her of the traumatic event.

Trauma could profoundly affect one's body (e.g., amygdala, hippocampus, autonomic nervous system). After trauma, a person may become very sensitive and hyperaroused; his/her stress response systems are also affected, and he/she may have difficulty in relaxing or getting to sleep.

Trauma leaves a person with unprocessed memories and unaddressed emotions, which may become nightmares or lead to flashbacks.

It should be noted that while stressful events are not always traumatic, chronic or extreme stress may have similar consequences as well.

What is dissociation? How is it related to trauma?

In fact, dissociation is an important concept in understanding traumatization.

Dissociation refers to a failure in integrating certain biopsychosocial experiences within the personality system. These biopsychosocial experiences could be memories, emotions, behaviors, visual images, motor control, aspects of identity and so on.

Dissociative experiences are common and can be very normal. For example: daydreaming, forgetfulness, being unaware of others talking around you when focusing on reading a book.

However, some people may suffer from pathological dissociation. Examples of pathological dissociation include psychological amnesia, being unable to recognize oneself in the mirror, flashbacks of painful memories and identity dissociation (having two or more distinct identities/ personality states).

As mentioned, trauma occurs when a person is overwhelmed to the point that he/she cannot process and integrate the experience of the event – that is to say, he/she has already dissociated. Now you will find out why dissociation is related to trauma.

When a person is traumatized, he/she is unable to process and integrate the experience. For example, he/she may feel numb and have no feelings, he/she may feel like the body's reactions (e.g., shaking) are uncontrollable; or he/she may not even be able to recall the memory of the event. These all involve dissociation.

Dissociation basically means disconnection. A person can be disconnected from thoughts, feelings, memories, sensations or any aspect of the mind or body. Dissociation can be a helpful survival strategy, but it can also cause problems if it persists after the trauma is over.

The nature of a traumatic event, when it happens, how many times it happens, whether there is enough social support and care after trauma.... these all could affect the impact of trauma and the level of dissociation.

In the case of a mature adult who grew up in a caring family, after a single car accident, he/she may have nightmares and flashbacks and not be able to remember the details of the accident. However, he/she continues to have a basically integrated personality and his/her post-traumatic and dissociative symptoms are not very severe; only some traumatic memories and trauma-related emotions are dissociated.

In the case of a young child whose personality is still developing, chronic family violence may seriously disrupt the child's process of integrating his/her experiences. His/her personality system may become highly dissociated. He/she may have multiple dissociated personality states – each part having a different sense of self (identity), holding certain emotions and memories, and being responsible for certain functions. He/she may suffer from severe pathological dissociation as well as other psychological symptoms.

You can see that, if the trauma is more intense, more frequent, more long-lasting and starts earlier in life, the consequences will be more serious. So, we have discussed how trauma could affect us and the concept of dissociation.

The impacts of trauma can be very profound, but the possibility of recovering from trauma is very good. The impacts of trauma are often reversible. Now let's discuss why you should remain hopeful.

First, there have already been many successful stories in which survivors recovered very well and had a wonderful life after trauma. Well-known survivors include: the famous singer, Madonna; the past president of the Asia Society, Robert Oxnam; Chris Costner Sizemore, the real Eve of *The Three Faces of Eve*; and Nobel Peace Prize Laureate, Malala.

Second, after many years of scientific studies and clinical experience, there are evidence-based treatments for trauma. There are clinical guidelines for treating trauma and dissociation. For instance, the International Society for Traumatic Stress Studies (ISTSS) developed the *ISTSS Expert Consensus Treatment Guidelines for Complex PTSD in Adults* in 2012, and the International Society for the Study of Trauma and Dissociation (ISSTD) developed the *Guidelines for Treating Dissociative Identity Disorder in Adults, Third Revision* in 2011.

Third, our brains are plastic, which means the human brain is malleable and we are able to change our brains. While unpleasant experiences (e.g., trauma, stress) can affect a person biologically, other experiences can also change his/her brain and neurological systems. Through learning, treatment, exercise and positive social interactions, everyone can change their brain too. For example, research shows that practicing mindfulness and psychotherapy can lead to biological changes. Thus, trauma is reversible. Recovery is always possible.

You may ask: how do I recover from trauma then?

As the impacts of trauma are real, you cannot simply 'forget about it' and then move on in your life. If the post-traumatic and dissociative reactions continue and affect your life, it means you cannot not just ignore the trauma.

To reverse the impacts of trauma, there are some principles:

- Ensure safety, prevent new trauma and stay away from chronic stress
- Look for social support and professional services
- Acknowledge the impacts of trauma
- Master the skills to cope with the symptoms
- Understand the meanings/reasons behind the symptoms, use harmless alternatives to replace the maladaptive behaviors
- Respect and accept every part of yourself (never try to eliminate any part of you!!!!)
- Process the traumatic memories and integrate your dissociated parts only when you are ready and when you have enough support – never force yourself
- Go slow, don't rush

Assignment 4.1

Have you experienced some unpleasant events that have had an impact on you? Could you try to write down how the event(s) affected your life? You do not need to talk about the details of the event(s).

Assignment 4.2

Recovery from trauma is always possible. Your efforts are important. A supportive environment is also very helpful. Could you identify some factors (e.g., strengths, resources) that could increase your chance of recovery? You can include both internal and external factors.

Question 1: Does the content in this chapter relate to your experience?
1 = Strongly disagree; 10 = Strongly agree

Question 2: Have you learned this content before?
1 = Strongly disagree; 10 = Strongly agree

Chapter 5: Common Reactions To Trauma And Stress

This chapter aims to:

1. Enable readers to be familiar with the common post-traumatic and dissociative reactions
2. Discuss the potential link between mental health problems and trauma

Trauma and chronic stress are related to various mental health problems, including depression, psychosis, behavioral problems, pathological dissociation and post-traumatic reactions. Every person is unique. Different people respond to trauma and stress differently. Different survivors may have different difficulties.

This chapter introduces some post-traumatic and dissociative reactions that are common among survivors. It should be noted that there are many different ways to categorize these symptoms.

Avoidance

After trauma and extreme stress, a person may try very hard to avoid remembering the painful event. He/she may want to avoid certain people, things or places. The person may not want to talk about the event again. He/she may also use a lot of strategies to keep himself/herself away from the painful feelings. Some people may make themselves very busy in the office so that they have no time to think of the traumatic events. Some people may use alcohol or drugs to avoid their negative emotions. Additionally, some people may avoid sleeping to prevent nightmares too.

While avoidance can be a helpful way to protect a person from being harmed again, it can also lead to many problems in his/her life. After you learn how to ground yourself back to the present moment and integrate your traumatized parts, avoidance symptoms should be reduced.

Hypervigilance

After a traumatic event, a person may become very sensitive, easily overreacting to sounds or small things. As mentioned in the previous chapter, trauma can disturb a person's physiological systems, especially the autonomic nervous system. It is like the fire alarm inside your body is not working – it keeps beeping even when there is no real danger.

People with hypervigilance may be easily angered, irritable or scared, may have sleep problems, and may have difficulty in concentration.

When a traumatized person is highly vigilant, he/she may be worried about being hurt by other people close to him/her. This could lead to social conflict.

While some medications might be helpful for some people, you will need to consult your doctor and see if one works for you.

Perhaps, you can also make a plan for yourself: what do you think you want to do when you are irritated or triggered? Can you think of a 3-step or 4-step plan for yourself so that you can follow the plan when you are about to overreact in the future? For example, the plan for preventing overreacting may include the following 3 steps:

1) breathe deeply 5 times
2) go drink some water
3) think of an alternative response to overreaction

We are not sure if these strategies will work for you, but they are worth a try. You can also practice your plan by rehearsal.

In addition, practicing mindfulness can be very beneficial. If you practice mindfulness (e.g., mindful breathing) in daily life, you will be more able to hold on for a while and take a deep breath when you are irritated or triggered. This step could give you a chance to think differently, e.g., have you misunderstood someone or something? Is this just a small problem? Did you overreact? Can you think about the situation in a different way?

Intrusive symptoms

Intrusive symptoms refer to those psychophysiological experiences (e.g., memories, emotions, behaviors, physiological feelings, ideas, mental images) that involuntarily intrude into one's consciousness. They in fact belong to you, but trauma and stress make you unable to integrate them as parts of your subjective experience.

Intrusions are the flip side of disconnection. The disconnected thoughts, feelings, memories or impulses get triggered and suddenly flood back in. Flashbacks are a form of intrusive symptoms in which the disconnected memories of past trauma get triggered and involuntarily intrude into a person's consciousness. This is why flashbacks are referred to as dissociative reactions or dissociative flashbacks. They are an intrusion from the past.

Besides, intrusions may also come from a person's inner teammates or inner members – they may be sending out some messages in the form of voices, emotions, visuals or even body sensations.

For example, some people may have flashbacks of painful memories, may feel like they are having emotions or feelings that do not belong to them, may hear voices inside their heads (e.g., voices commenting on their behaviors), may have done something but feel like it was not what they wanted to do, or may have some strange impulsive thoughts. An extreme but not rare example of intrusive symptoms is hallucinations – you see, hear or feel something that does not exist in the external world.

Emotions, feelings and symptoms do not come without reasons. Very often, there are reasons/meanings behind these experiences. Intrusive symptoms are the same. Intrusive symptoms sometimes can be seen as messages or reminders that our body and mind give us. If you have intrusive symptoms, it may feel like these experiences do not belong to you, but you need to know that they are basically parts of you. They are just dissociated from you.

In the long term, you will need to find out the reasons/meanings behind the intrusive symptoms. You will need to gradually accept and integrate these experiences. To do so, you probably need an experienced therapist to support you.

However, there are also some methods for you to manage intrusive symptoms on your own. Grounding techniques are powerful ways to help you handle flashbacks, panic attacks and other intrusive symptoms that make you feel pain in the present. Likewise, self-talk can be helpful too. For instance, when you have intrusive symptoms, you may talk to yourself, e.g., "I was hurt in the past, but I am safe now, I am capable of protecting myself now, relax," or "Thank you for sending me this message, I know you are suffering, can we peacefully discuss how to help us suffer less?"

Try to be humble and open, listen to your inner parts. They may give you feedback when appropriate.

We will further discuss how to cope with intrusive symptoms in Chapter 10.

Interpersonal difficulties

Interpersonal problems are not rare in people who have experienced trauma and stress, especially if it is childhood interpersonal trauma (e.g., physical abuse, emotional neglect, family violence).

For many childhood trauma survivors, their parents could not be good role models to demonstrate how to regulate their own emotions, how to interact respectfully with other people, and how to maintain a stable relationship. Therefore, these survivors could not learn how to handle interpersonal conflicts or set healthy interpersonal boundaries.

After trauma, some people may not be able to trust other people because they have been hurt. Some survivors may have unstable emotions that increase the chance of having social conflicts too.

If you keep having interpersonal problems, there are some important things that you may want to remember:

- protect yourself, stay away from abusive or toxic relationships
- learn how to reject unreasonable demands from others
- reflect on whether you have reasonable expectations of others
- reflect on whether you are repeating some unhealthy relationship patterns
- reflect on how your past may affect your ways of interacting with other people
- set healthy interpersonal boundaries
- consider whether it would be better to use text messages instead of face-to-face conversations to avoid conflicts when you are emotionally unstable
- apologize after you have done something rude due to unstable emotions or intrusive symptoms

We will further discuss how to handle interpersonal problems in Chapter 11.

Cognitive distortions

As mentioned in Chapter 4, trauma could affect our thinking process – the way we think about ourselves, the way we think about other people, and the way we think about the world. Cognitive distortions can result in emotional problems and interpersonal conflicts.

For example, some survivors may think that they do not feel worthy of being loved; some survivors may think they are responsible for the unhappy event; and, some survivors may start to believe that people come close only for hurting them. These beliefs 'learned' after the trauma are somehow protective in nature but could also lead to many difficulties in the recovery journey.

Do you think you have any cognitive distortions? To correct these irrational thinking patterns, you need to be familiar with them, recognize them and challenge them.

One potentially helpful technique is to think from a scientist's perspective: Imagine you are a scientist, when you see an event or a phenomenon (e.g., a conversation with your friend, an action of your colleague, a minor conflict with someone on the street), how would you interpret it? What conclusion would you come to? Do you have any evidence to support your conclusion? Is there any other explanation?

You can practice this technique in your everyday life.

We will further discuss how to identify and handle cognitive distortions in Chapter 7.

Dissociative amnesia

Memory problems, in particular dissociative amnesia, may also occur in some trauma survivors. These memory problems are not caused by drugs, alcohol or other physical reasons (e.g., brain injury). For instance, a survivor may not remember what happened during the traumatic event or could not recall some of the details. For some survivors who have more severe pathological dissociation, they may even have 'time loss' or 'memory gaps' in their everyday life. Examples of dissociative amnesia may include:

- A person is told that he/she has done something, but he/she does not remember doing so
- A person 'wakes up' and suddenly realizes that he/she is in a strange place where he/she does not remember how he/she get there
- A person finds some strange objects (e.g., books, handouts, drawings, clothes, toys) at home but he/she does not know where the things came from
- A person realizes that he/she has lost his/her memory for a period of time (e.g., several hours, days or even months)

Dissociative amnesia usually occurs because something is too overwhelming to the point that the conscious mind is not ready to process the memories. This is protective in nature.

If a person's personality dissociates to a certain degree, he/she may have amnesia for other experiences in daily life as well. This is because other dissociated personality states of the person hold the memories and do not yet share the memories with the person (see 'identity dissociation' discussed below).

Dissociative amnesia may sound like a serious problem, but you do not need to worry so much. It usually responds well to dissociation-focused psychotherapy. Also, there are some ways you can cope with dissociative amnesia.

You do not need to force yourself to remember. Your memories will come back at an appropriate time (e.g., after you feel safe enough, or after you are fully ready to know what happened).

If you have frequent dissociative amnesia in your daily life, you may try to write in your journal regularly. Many people recommend this practice. This could let your dissociated personality states know what's going on.

It could also give you a chance to receive messages from your 'internal family members' – they may write to you as well.

In addition, it would be very helpful if you could get support from someone who you can trust. A reliable friend or family member could probably help you solve some of the problems caused by your amnesia.

Also, you can keep a calendar to note down important dates and what you will need to do in the future. This could remind you and your dissociated personality states to do appropriate things even if there are memory gaps. In the long term, when you are fully ready, you will be able to face, process and accept the dissociated memories. It is also possible to reduce memory gaps in daily life by connecting and cooperating with your internal family members.

We will further discuss how to cope with dissociative amnesia in Chapter 10.

Depersonalization and Derealization

Depersonalization refers to the experience of feeling detached from the self, and one's thoughts, feelings, sensations or actions, or feeling unreal or absent (e.g., you could not recognize yourself in a mirror, you feel like you are acting as a robot, you feel that your emotions do not belong to you, or you feel like you are watching yourself as if you are an outside observer).

Derealization refers to the experience of feeling unreal or feeling detached from outside surroundings (e.g., people or things are unreal, dreamlike, foggy, lifeless or visually distorted).

Depersonalization and derealization may occur in people who are experiencing trauma, stress or anxiety. These two types of experience are not always pathological, unless they occur frequently and make you feel very unconformable or result in difficulty in work or social interactions. While professional treatment is probably needed when you suffer from prolonged depersonalization/derealization, you may try to reduce the symptoms by staying away from stressors and triggers.

You can also use grounding techniques or breathing exercises to cope with depersonalization/derealization.

Some people may think that physical pain could make them feel 'real' again. However, making yourself experience physical pain could be a harmful way to cope. Instead of hurting yourself, you could try to have some type of safe sensory stimulation (e.g., touch some ice cubes for a while). This could probably help you reconnect with reality.

Somatic symptoms (somatoform dissociation)

Somatic symptoms – or medically unexplained physical symptoms – are very common among people with mental health problems, especially in traumatized populations.

For example:

- Pain symptoms (e.g., headache, stomach ache, back pain) without physical causes
- Temporary or chronic physical impairments (e.g., visual impairment, deafness, difficulty in speaking, difficulty in walking) without physical causes

Some people with somatic symptoms may also present with problems such as diarrhea, vomiting, seizures or fainting when no physical causes can be found.

Sometimes somatic symptoms are the body's response to trauma and stress. Some scholars believe that somatic symptoms also involve dissociation (known as somatoform dissociation) – there is a disconnection or dissociation between the mind and the body. Somatic symptoms may be caused by dissociated personality states too – the personality states willingly or unwillingly cause physical symptoms for psychological reasons (e.g., unprocessed traumatic memories related to physical abuse). In some cases, somatic symptoms may also hold 'meaning' (e.g., a survivor presents with back pain during Christmas every year because he/she had been physically abused during a Christmas holiday in the past).

If you have any physical symptoms or problems, the most important thing is to find out first whether there is any physical cause. You need to consult your medical doctor.

If you have somatic symptoms and physical causes have been ruled out through a comprehensive medical assessment, an experienced therapist could probably assist you to find out the underlying reasons/meanings.

When coping with somatic symptoms, intrusive symptoms or other dissociative symptoms, you need to be humble and open-minded. Try to listen to your mind – is there any message your internal family members want you to know? It is possible to reduce somatic symptoms by taking care of the needs of your internal family members.

You could also manage somatic symptoms by using distraction, actively changing your emotions, or identifying and challenging your cognitive distortions or negative thoughts. Different strategies may work for different people.

Identity dissociation

Identity dissociation is a less commonly used term. Here it refers to the dissociation of a person's identity.

When a person's personality dissociates as a result of trauma or extreme stress, the dissociated part may be an emotion, a memory or a motor control function, or a combination of these. While the dissociated parts may be fragments, it is also possible that the dissociated part is a personality state (also called an identity state) that has an independent identity (sense of self).

A dissociated personality state may have his/her own identity (or even name), gender, psychological age, memories, thinking patterns, behavioral styles, abilities, interests or even physiological features (e.g., brain activity).

A person who has been severely traumatized may have many dissociated personality states in addition to many personality fragments. This may or may not co-occur with recurrent dissociative amnesia. If this internal psychological structure exists, and if it leads to significant distress or impairment, the condition is called 'dissociative identity disorder' (DID), which was previously known as 'multiple personality disorder' (MPD) or sometimes is called split personality.

In fact, everyone has only one personality, no matter if you have dissociated or not. Your personality is the sum of all the parts within your personality (including those dissociated parts, if any).

Identity dissociation could lead to identity alteration. Identity alteration is a commonly used term that refers to alteration from one identity to another identity. This is often called 'switching' – it occurs when another personality state takes over control of the body.

Everyone experiences normal identity alteration in daily life: we behave differently when seeing a friend compared to when meeting our boss.

However, in the case of a person who has identity dissociation after trauma or extreme stress, he/she cannot always control his/her identity alteration, and he/she may also have problems associated with identity alteration (e.g., he/she does not have the memories of the other identities, he/she cannot manage or control when to assume which identities).

As mentioned above, some people refer to identity alteration as switching of personalities.

Examples of identity alteration (as an observable symptom of identity dissociation) may include:

1) An adult suddenly behaves and speaks as if he/she is a child (known as age regression)

2) A person refers to himself/herself by a strange or new name

3) A person responds completely differently to the same thing

These observable behaviors correspond to the person feeling as if there is another person or another self in his/her mind and the person inside is influencing him/her, or even controlling his/her behaviors (e.g., actions, speech).

If you have identity dissociation, your goal will be to live peacefully with your dissociated personality states, acknowledge them, respect them, accept them and cooperate with them. However, this takes time and you need to do it gradually.

We use the term 'internal family members' to describe the dissociated personality states because we want to emphasize the importance of mutual respect and care. To recover from trauma and extreme stress, you will need to have good teamwork with your dissociated parts (whether or not they are fully dissociated).

Writing a welcoming or grateful letter to your dissociated parts may be a great start.

If you cannot communicate with them yet, writing messages or letters could be helpful (some people even use voice recordings to pass messages to other dissociated personality states).

If you are already able to communicate with them, show your respect, acknowledge their contributions and efforts in protecting you and themselves, and try to understand them (including their needs).

As Thich Nhat Hanh said, "Everything is possible when the door of communication is open."

We will further discuss how to cope with dissociative amnesia in Chapter 10.

Assignment 5.1

Do you have any of the symptoms mentioned in this chapter? If yes, could you select one symptom, write down how it affects you and how you plan to manage this in the future?

Assignment 5.2

Have you tried any of the coping strategies described in this chapter? If so, which ones have worked the best?

Question 1: Does the content in this chapter relate to your experience?
1 = Strongly disagree; 10 = Strongly agree

Question 2: Have you learned this content before?
1 = Strongly disagree; 10 = Strongly agree

Chapter 6: Trauma-Related Mental Disorders: What Do These Labels Mean?

This chapter aims to:

1. Introduce some psychiatric diagnoses commonly related to trauma

2. Discuss the pros and cons of using psychiatric labels

The world is complicated. Human behaviors are also complicated. In a society, we need systems and categories to classify phenomena that we observe. This enables us to describe, talk about and investigate various phenomena. Category systems are constructed by us based on our understanding, culture and research. Category systems can be very helpful for knowledge development, but they are just systems for labelling things. They may not always be always accurate.

In the field of mental health, *Diagnostic and Statistical Manual of Mental Disorders (DSM)* and *International Statistical Classification of Diseases and Related Health Problems (ICD)* are the two diagnostic systems most commonly used internationally. The DSM is published by the American Psychiatric Association and has been updated to its fifth edition in 2013 (known as DSM-5). The ICD is released by the World Health Organization (WHO) and it came into its eleventh edition (known as ICD-11) in 2018. These two manuals provide guidelines for clinical practitioners and researchers to assess and diagnose mental health problems. There are some similarities in these two diagnostic systems, but they are not the same.

It is not uncommon for a patient to meet the diagnostic criteria for more than one mental disorder. Since trauma and stress can affect a person in many ways, comorbidity (i.e., having two or more disorders at the same time) is particularly common among trauma survivors. For example, a person may be diagnosed with major depressive disorder, post-traumatic stress disorder and borderline personality disorder at the same time.

There are some psychiatric diagnoses commonly related to trauma.

Acute stress disorder (ASD) is a psychiatric diagnosis describing post-traumatic reactions occurring between 3 days and one month after experiencing a traumatic event. These reactions may include intrusive symptoms (e.g., flashbacks, distressing dreams, painful memories), negative mood, dissociative symptoms (e.g., amnesia), avoidance symptoms and arousal symptoms. There are specific diagnostic criteria for ASD in the DSM-5. ASD has been included as an official diagnosis in the DSM since 1994. According to the DSM-5, studies showed that ASD tends to be identified in less than 20% of survivors of non-interpersonal trauma (e.g., motor vehicle accidents, severe burns), whereas survivors of interpersonal trauma (e.g., assault, rape) are a bit more likely to suffer from ASD. Some people with ASD develop PTSD at a later time.

Post-traumatic stress disorder (PTSD) is a mental disorder commonly found in trauma survivors. PTSD used to be known as 'shell shock' or 'combat neurosis' and has been officially recognized in the DSM since 1980. PTSD develops in some persons who have been exposed to a traumatic event (e.g. serious injury, abuse, violence, serious accident, war). A person with PTSD may have directly experienced the trauma, witnessed the trauma of another person, and/or learned that the trauma occurred to a close person. Patients with PTSD typically present with intrusive symptoms, avoidance symptoms, cognitive and mood symptoms, and arousal and reactivity symptoms. The symptoms last at least one month. There are specific diagnostic criteria for PTSD in the DSM-5. While medications may be helpful for patients with PTSD, trauma-focused psychotherapies are the first-line treatments for PTSD. For instance, the effectiveness of prolonged exposure (PE) therapy, cognitive processing therapy (CPT), cognitive behavioral therapy (CBT) and eye movement desensitization and reprocessing (EMDR) for PTSD is supported by many clinical studies. These treatments are also strongly recommended by the American Psychological Association (2017)'s and/ or Veterans Affairs (VA)/Department of Defense (DoD) Clinical Practice Guideline Working Group (2017)'s treatment guidelines for PTSD.

Some scholars have long suggested that the impacts of a single trauma and chronic trauma (e.g., family violence, child abuse) can be very different in terms of their clinical presentations and the treatments needed. Therefore, after a long period of research and advocacy, **complex PTSD** became an official diagnosis in the ICD-11 in 2018. In addition to PTSD symptoms, patients with complex PTSD can have other problems, such as difficulties in affect regulation, negative beliefs and interpersonal problems, and dissociative symptoms. In DSM-5 there is a dissociative subtype of PTSD characterized by symptoms of depersonalization and derealisation. Treatments for simple PTSD may not be suitable or enough for complex PTSD. Experts in the field recommend a phase-based treatment approach for complex PTSD. The treatment usually consists of three major phases: (1) ensuring safety and reducing symptoms, (2) processing trauma, and (3) consolidating treatment gains.

Borderline personality disorder (BPD) is a personality disorder characterized by impulsivity and a chronic instability in interpersonal relationships, sense of self, and emotions and marked impulsivity. For example, some patients with BPD may chronically suffer from unstable interpersonal relationships, impulsivity and risk-taking behaviors, fear of abandonment and/or poor emotional management. There are specific diagnostic criteria for BPD in the DSM-5. According to the DSM-5, the prevalence of BPD may be between 1.6% to 5.9% in the general population. BPD is even more common among mental health service users. Studies have shown that BPD is closely associated with childhood trauma. Some scholars believe that BPD should be understood as a trauma disorder. There is evidence that suggests that specialized psychotherapies are effective in treating BPD.

Dissociative disorders include several mental disorders characterized by pathological dissociation, although some other mental disorders (e.g., ASD, PTSD, complex PTSD, BPD) also involve pathological dissociation to a certain degree. In the DSM-5, there are several different dissociative disorders: (1) dissociative amnesia, (2) depersonalization/derealization disorder, (3) dissociative identity disorder, (4) other specified dissociative disorder, and (5) unspecified dissociative disorder. Each of them has specific diagnostic criteria.

Dissociative amnesia (DA) is characterized by psychological amnesia – an inability to recall important autobiographical information (e.g., unable to recall a traumatic or stressful event, amnesia for a period of time, loss of memory for certain personal information).

Depersonalization/derealization disorder (DPD) is characterized by depersonalization (disconnected or detached from yourself) and/or derealization (disconnected or detached from your environment), which have been introduced in Chapter 5.

Dissociative identity disorder (DID), previously known as multiple personality disorder (MPD), is characterized by dissociative amnesia and identity alteration. People with DID typically have two or more distinct personality states, which may have different identities, interests, abilities, gender, age and behavioral patterns. A person with DID will have dissociative amnesia to a certain degree (e.g., cannot remember some traumatic experiences, cannot remember what other personality states have done, loss of memory for a period[s] of time). In some cultures, the symptoms of DID may be described as an experience of possession. International studies suggest that the prevalence of DID may be around 1% in the general population. DID is more common among psychiatric patients. Almost all patients with DID have encountered certain adversities (e.g., physical abuse, verbal abuse, family violence, emotional neglect) in their lives, especially during childhood. DID can be understood as the most severe form of post-traumatic mental disorder. Although medications may be helpful for short-term symptom management, phase-based psychotherapy is the primary treatment for DID. The treatment usually consists of three major phases: (1) safety and stabilization, (2) trauma processing, and (3) integration. Treatment should acknowledge the impacts of trauma, respect all parts of the patient (including all other personality states), and aim at achieving internal (inter-personality) communication and cooperation. There is evidence that suggests that patients with DID respond very well to specialized psychotherapy.

Other specified dissociative disorder (OSDD) is a diagnosis used to describe those patients who have dissociative symptoms resulting in significant distress or impairment in daily life but who do not fully meet the diagnostic criteria for any other dissociative disorder. For example, a patient with OSDD may have several distinct personality states but not have dissociative amnesia.

In some cases, OSDD may be seen as a less severe form of DID. DID and OSDD have similar or common features. Therefore, some scholars use the term 'complex dissociative disorders', or 'chronic complex dissociative disorders', to describe DID and OSDD. Among various psychiatric diagnostic groups, patients with complex dissociative disorders report the highest frequency of childhood abuse.

Unspecified dissociative disorder is a diagnosis that may be used by a clinician when there is not enough information to make a more specific diagnosis.

The above-mentioned psychiatric diagnoses are closely related to trauma, and therefore they are widely recognized as trauma-related disorders. However, this does not mean that other psychiatric diagnoses (e.g., major depressive disorder, panic disorder, schizophrenia) are not related to trauma.

Again, it is not uncommon for trauma survivors to present with various mental health problems (e.g., dissociation, depression, anxiety, substance abuse, psychosis), and thus meet the diagnostic criteria for a number of different disorders.

For instance, most patients with DID suffer from major depression, more than half of patients with DID meet criteria for some type of psychotic disorder, and half or more of patients with DID meet criteria for BPD as well. A person with DID who meets criteria for a psychotic disorder is usually not actually psychotic; symptoms like voices, which are actually dissociative in nature (the voices of other identity states) are incorrectly classified as psychotic symptoms by many psychiatrists, by DSM-5 criteria and by research measures for psychosis. There is evidence that approximately half of patients with PTSD also suffer from major depression.

While you may now have some more ideas about what these psychiatric labels mean, there are several things to be aware of.

1. **Correct diagnosis is important:** Early identification and correct diagnosis are important because the diagnosis could affect the treatment plan. The common understanding is that different diagnoses require different treatments. For example, if a patient has psychosis or schizophrenia, antipsychotic medications may be preferred; if the patient has depression, antidepressant medications or cognitive-behavioral therapy (CBT) may be preferred. For many clinicians, trauma-focused psychotherapy may be considered only when the patient has a trauma-related disorder (e.g., PTSD). If a patient with PTSD or DID is misdiagnosed as having only depression, specialized psychotherapy may not be offered to him/her. Therefore, correct diagnosis is important.

2. **Diagnosis cannot reflect your real life:** Although diagnosis is important from a clinical perspective, this is after all just a label. A diagnostic label cannot tell who you are, what you have experienced, how you feel and what you need. Although two different people with the same diagnosis may share some similar or common features (e.g., similar symptom presentations), everyone is unique. You are also unique. Therefore, there is no need to care too much about diagnostic labels. You and your future are not defined by your diagnosis.

3. **The situation is not always clear:** There can be many challenges in the diagnostic process. In some cases, the symptom presentations are complicated (e.g., having many different symptoms at the same time, and the psychiatrist only pays attention to the most obvious problems (e.g., depression) and overlooks other problems (e.g., trauma, dissociation). Psychiatrists and psychologists may also have biases. For example, an expert in depression might be more likely to diagnose people with depression, while an expert in trauma psychology might be more aware of the PTSD symptoms. It is not rare to see a story like this:

A patient was diagnosed with depression and anxiety by one psychiatrist, then diagnosed with depression and PTSD by a second psychiatrist, and then diagnosed with other problems by a third psychiatrist. A sad but true reality is that the inter-rater reliability of making a psychiatric diagnosis is not very high. This means, even for the same patient, different psychiatrists may make different diagnoses – diagnoses are not always consistent. For example, in many places, patients with DID are diagnosed with other problems (e.g., depression, psychosis) because not many psychiatrists are familiar with the diagnosis of DID. Therefore, diagnosis is important, but there is no need to care too much about a diagnostic label. In addition, if possible, try to seek a second opinion about your mental health problems from a different psychiatrist or clinical psychologist. If you think you have experienced certain traumatic or very stressful events or if you have some trauma-related mental health problems, you may seek help from a psychiatrist or clinical psychologist who is specialized in trauma therapy. If you are worried that you have dissociative symptoms, you may seek help from a psychiatrist or clinical psychologist who has specialized in dissociative disorders. If you have concerns about your diagnosis and treatment, you may also consider talking to your social worker – your social worker may be willing to go to a consultation with you so that you can have better communication with your psychiatrist or clinical psychologist.

No matter what disorder you have been diagnosed with, don't let the diagnosis define you and your life. It is still very possible for you to improve your health, enjoy your life and embrace a good future. You can do a lot of things for your own good: eat well, sleep enough, exercise, connect with people, talk to others, practice mindfulness, learn new things, get professional support and so on.

Assignment 6.1

There are ups and downs in our mental health. It can be affected by what happens around us. By reviewing your past experience, can you find out in what situations you could have better mental health in the future?

Assignment 6.2

Your life is not defined by your mental health problems. What do you want to do when you have recovered from your mental health problems?

Question 1: Does the content in this chapter relate to your experience?
1 = Strongly disagree; 10 = Strongly agree

Question 2: Have you learned this content before?
1 = Strongly disagree; 10 = Strongly agree

Chapter 7: Irrational Thoughts

This chapter aims to:

1. Introduce some common irrational thoughts in our everyday thinking
2. Enable readers to identify and avoid irrational thoughts

Irrational thoughts are common in our everyday lives. There may be reasons for these irrational thoughts (e.g., your past experience, what you have learned from others), but you should not ignore them. Your thoughts can affect your emotions and behaviors. Therefore, it is important for you to identify and change your irrational thoughts. Correcting irrational thoughts is also one of the core components of cognitive-behavioral psychotherapy (CBT). This chapter introduces several common irrational thoughts and discusses how we could correct these errors in thinking.

Overgeneralization means that a person makes a broad conclusion based on a single incident or limited observations. This kind of thinking makes us unable to be open-minded about different possibilities in new situations.

> Example 1: After a boy was hurt on one night, he started to believe that every night is dangerous.
>
> Example 2: After observing how her parents got divorced, a girl thinks that it is impossible to have a successful marriage.

Catastrophizing means that a person thinks only of the worst situation. This kind of irrational thought makes us overestimate the likelihood of the worst situation actually occurring.

> Example 1: When a boy gets sick, his mother keeps thinking that her son may have a certain serious illness that could lead to his death.
>
> Example 2: A lady may believe that she will be abandoned if she expresses any anger.

Polarized thinking, also known as 'black or white' thinking, means a person sees things only in extremes. This kind of irrational thought makes us unable to see the shades of gray and achieve balance.

> Example 1: A boy thinks his parents can only be either good or bad parents and cannot stand that his 'good' parents have made mistakes.
>
> Example 2: A girl believes that everyone who does not love her hates her.

Locus of control shift means that a person uses magical thinking to shift responsibility to himself/herself in an attempt to gain some power and control in a situation of powerlessness and helplessness. This kind of irrational thought makes us feel as if we still have some control, but also makes us unable to see the reality of the situation, namely that we do not have control over it.

> Example 1: A boy believes that if he had been good enough, his parents would not have divorced.
>
> Example 2: A girl thinks that she was abused because she had done something wrong.

Confirmation bias means a person uses information selectively or interprets information in a biased way so as to confirm his/her pre-existing beliefs. This kind of irrational thought makes it easy to reach an incorrect conclusion.

> Example 1: Even if a boy has been chronically abused by his father, he only thinks of how his father brought him a toy in order to support his belief that his father loves him so much.
>
> Example 2: When a father is angry with his daughter, he focuses solely on the bad things she has done and does not remember what good things she has done before.

Demandingness beliefs means that a person holds beliefs that things 'should', 'must' or 'have to' happen in a certain way. This kind of irrational thought makes us have unreasonable expectations of ourselves, other people and other things.

> Example 1: A mother thinks that her children must have good achievements at school.
>
> Example 2: A boy thinks that he should not cry in order to be a good person.

All of us have irrational thoughts from time to time. These thoughts are often negative and unrealistic. Irrational thoughts are sometimes harmless and sometimes harmful. For instance, if you irrationally believe that you are responsible for your friend's accident, you may feel guilty; if you have unreasonably high expectations of your close friends, it may hurt those friendships.

People may also develop irrational thoughts after encountering traumatic or very stressful experiences. Some examples are as follows:

> A young woman thinks that her boyfriend will hurt her just like her father and ex-boyfriends, and therefore she cannot develop a trusting relationship with her boyfriend. She overgeneralizes her experiences in the past and cannot see the possibility that her

boyfriend is an exception.

A boy thinks that he is the one to blame because his parents and siblings abused him; he believes that if he had been a good, lovely child, they would not have done that. He feels helpless and powerless at home. What he can do is believe that he is responsible for the abuse; if he is the one who made the abuse happen, then he can gain some sense of control even in a very uncontrollable situation.

A male personality part in a person with DID argues that he must be aggressive and strong in order to protect himself because the host personality is very weak and could not stand the pain in the past. He only concentrates on what happened in the past and does not recognize that the host personality may be very mature and strong now.

A wife who has been experiencing family violence for a long time still wants to stay with her abusive husband. "It's just bad temper. He has had a difficult time in his career recently. He still loves me so much. You see, he usually buys new things for me." The wife tries to rationalize his violence.

A patient does not want to interact with his internal personality parts because he thinks that they must be uncooperative. Such a demandingness belief may be based on the fact that he is worried about facing the traumatic memories that the alters hold.

A girl has been rejected many times. No one wants to listen to her. No one acknowledges her experiences. She starts to believe that she does not need anyone and that she can do everything herself. In order not to be rejected again, she chooses to believe that she does not need help from others and decides not to seek help again. Her past experiences of being rejected are painful. They make her unable to acknowledge the fact that everyone needs help from time to time. Perhaps, though, she would not be rejected again next time if she took some risks in future relationships.

A trauma survivor believes that he can never get well, and that life is full of pain. He has such beliefs because of his past experience. He cannot acknowledge the fact that everything has changed – the traumatic event is no longer happening, he has grown up and can protect himself now, and it is always possible for him to suffer less and recover from trauma.

Irrational thoughts negatively affect how we feel and how we respond to a situation.

Emotions and thoughts are always interacting with each other. For example, when you are angry or nervous, you may have more negative thoughts; when you think in a negative way, you may also have more negative emotions.

If you are emotionally unstable and have irrational thoughts, calm yourself down first. You need to use the skills you have learned (e.g., grounding techniques, mindful breathing) to regulate your emotions first. It is difficult to think rationally when you are emotionally unstable. After you have calmed down, it is more likely that you can be reflective.

To correct irrational thoughts, the primary step is to identify them.

You need to practice. Identify your irrational thoughts in your daily life. You may want to have a daily journal so that you can review some of your irrational thoughts. This could make you become a more reflective person.

To avoid irrational thoughts, you can try the **Become-a-Scientist Exercise**, which has been introduced in Chapter 5. When you have a belief or an idea (e.g., "all men are dangerous" or "no one will trust me"), you need to think: do I have evidence to support my belief? Is the evidence reliable and strong enough? Are there any exceptions? Are there any alternative explanations for your observations? Is your conclusion directly supported by your observations? Have you overgeneralized your observations? If you can consider these issues carefully, it is very likely that you can avoid or reduce your irrational thoughts.

You can also try another exercise: **Debate with Yourself**. When you have a viewpoint or a statement (e.g., "I am a bad guy" or "my classmates bully me just because I have done something wrong"), write down two boxes – one box for the affirmative side, another box for the negative side. First, imagine that you are on the one side, list down as many points as possible to support your argument (e.g., "I am a bad guy" is true) in one box. After that, you speak on the negative side; list down as many points as possible to support your argument (e.g., "I am a bad guy" is false) in the other box. This could help you think of both sides of an argument and think in a less biased and more rational way.

However, it should be noted that if the irrational thoughts come from your dissociated personality states or internal family members, you should show your gratitude and respect for them first. Challenging them directly may be offensive to them, which is not good for internal harmony and internal cooperation. You may consider talking to them peacefully and discussing your viewpoints with them after you have built a good relationship with them.

Assignment 7.1

Try to identify an irrational thought that you have had recently. Do you know when and why you started having this irrational thought?

Assignment 7.2

It is important to view an issue from both sides. Think of a belief (e.g., "you should adopt a pet," or "you should find a new job"). Try to provide arguments and count-arguments for the belief.

Question 1: Does the content in this chapter relate to your experience?
1 = Strongly disagree; 10 = Strongly agree

Question 2: Have you learned this content before?
1 = Strongly disagree; 10 = Strongly agree

Chapter 8: Trauma Recovery And Integration Of The Personality

This chapter aims to:

1. Enable readers to be familiar with the direction for recovery
2. Explain why 'integration' is the goal of recovery
3. Review some important concepts related to trauma recovery

The journey of recovery is not always smooth and easy. Challenges may come from external and/or internal sources.

You may still be struggling in an early stage. You may be very distressed by your strange feelings and behaviors. You may be trying to understand the reasons behind your problems. You may already have learned some skills to manage your symptoms. Or, you may have started promoting internal harmony.

No matter which stage you are at now, you need to know your direction. Recovery can be a long process. You need to have determination. You also need to work hard. It is always important to avoid getting lost and confused. You need some kind of compass.

In order to help you avoid getting lost in the journey of recovery, this chapter explains what 'integration' means and why it is a key concept in trauma recovery. This can also help explain why 'be a teammate with yourself' is very important. In addition, this chapter also reviews some important concepts related to recovery.

Each person has a lot of different parts

Unlike what many people believe, there is no single 'self'. Everyone's personality is a complicated system. This personality system consists of many different parts (e.g., emotions, memories, beliefs, identities). The parts may exist at the conscious level or the unconscious level.

For example, you may have a part that is more child-like and has a great sense of fun and playfulness, and this part shows up when you are with your close friends; you may also have a part that is full of carefulness and nervousness and this part usually shows up when you are working with your boss or clients. Such parts are totally healthy and normal. Everything is under control.

As a person grows up and experiences new things every day, such experiences are integrated as parts of his/her personality.

Trauma interferes with the process of integration of the personality

Everyone has a lot of different parts. It is very normal to have parts.

Parts become problematic only when some normally accessible parts of you become inaccessible and when this leads to significant distress or impairment in your life. What does it mean that 'normally accessible parts become inaccessible'? Here are some examples:

- A person has an angry part, a frightened inner child or a depressed self that is very different from him/her and is out of control
- A person has some psychologically-induced physical symptoms (e.g., stomach ache, loss of voice)
- A person cannot access some of his/her important childhood memories
- A person cannot access his/her own feelings

In each of the above examples, the person could not access, connect to or use some psychophysiological functions or parts of the personality.

Why would this happen?

When a person encounters a traumatic or very stressful event, the process of integration of the personality may be interfered with.

You may already have understood that a traumatic event can overwhelm a person's ability to process and integrate the experiences (e.g., emotions, memories, motor controls) related to the event. To a certain degree, a traumatized person has a fragmented (dissociated) personality – he/ she disconnects from some parts (e.g., emotions, memories, identities, behaviors) of the personality.

In some cases (e.g., persons who have experienced one very stressful event, or patients with PTSD or BPD), only some limited parts of the personality are dissociated. For example:

- The person cannot remember some or all parts of the traumatic event (this is called dissociative amnesia)
- The person feels as if he/she is not the person who has encountered the trauma, or feels like a robot (this is called depersonalization)
- The person feels like the past trauma is happening again here and now (the dissociated trauma memories intrude into the consciousness) (this is called dissociative flashbacks)
- The person has difficulty having any emotions even when some very good or very bad things happen (this is called emotional numbness, which is also a form of disconnection

or depersonalization)

- The person is suddenly out of control of his/her body (e.g., cannot speak, cannot walk, cannot feel pain) even when there is no physical cause (this is called somatoform dissociation)

In some other cases (e.g., persons who have experienced chronic trauma, or patients with DID or OSDD), more parts of the personality are dissociated. In particular, the dissociated parts of the personality may have their own sense of self. For example:

- The person feels like there is an angry person inside and this angry person can significantly affect his/her life (e.g., comments on his/her actions harshly, forces him/her to do something, makes him/her to be angry even when he/she does not know why he/she feels angry)
- The person has amnesia for a number of life events, but he/she can recall such memories when he/she 'switches' to another identity state (e.g., a child personality)
- The person feels like there are several persons inside his/her mind and these persons have different names, genders, ages, interests, skills and memories

Integration is an important process in the journey towards recovery

Of course, a traumatized person could leave his or her fragmented mind untreated. A traumatized person could decide not to acknowledge, respect, face and accept the dissociated parts of the personality. However, this approach could cause problems.

The consequences of trauma-related dissociation of the personality have been discussed in some detail above. Examples of such problems include: flashbacks of painful memories, hearing voices from dissociated personality states, other intrusive symptoms (e.g., sudden compulsions, undesirable emotions), amnesic barriers, depersonalization, medically unexplained physical symptoms (somatoform dissociation), or inter-personality conflicts.

If a traumatized person wants to recover fully from trauma, he/she needs to process and integrate the dissociated parts, slowly, step by step. The dissociated parts may be: traumatic memories, painful emotions, or dissociated personality states.

Integration is not a process of eliminating the dissociated parts. Instead, integration is a process of recognizing, acknowledging, respecting, accepting, communicating with and cooperating with each part of the personality. It is about joining together, not getting rid of the parts.

If you have amnesia for a traumatic experience and it leads to significant distress or impairment in your life, your optimal goal would be processing and integrating the trauma memory as part of your own memory. Before you can do so, you need to do a number of things to make sure you are fully ready for trauma processing and personality integration. For example, you need to ensure safety (e.g., you need to avoid new trauma), learn healthy coping strategies (e.g., you need to know how to calm down your overreacting body), and you need to recognize the underlying needs behind your symptoms (e.g., you are depressed because you need to suppress your anger), acknowledge your dissociated parts (e.g., they have helped you survive by holding the pain for you) and show your acceptance and love for every part of you (e.g., your emotions, your feelings, your past, your various identities, your memories). Finally, you will be able to peacefully face and accept your traumatic experiences. Once you are fully ready, the inner mind will tell you what you need to know when the right time comes.

If you have flashbacks of painful memories and you want to reduce the symptom, your optimal goal would be processing and integrating the painful memories and related emotions. To do so, you first need to know how to use grounding techniques or other methods to feel safe. You also need to acknowledge the fact that some hidden part of you may have been seriously frightened – you need to accept, look after and comfort this part of you. With enough support (e.g., in psychotherapy), you will be able to face and process the painful memories slowly, step by step. By comforting the frightened part of you, you are also helping yourself to manage the flashbacks.

If you feel like you have a very depressed girl inside your mind and this part of you brings you trouble, your optimal goal should be integrating this depressed girl. Similarly, you also need to recognize the underlying needs of this depressed girl. You need to talk to her, respect her, thank her, work with her as a team, and support her to solve the very real problems (e.g., lack of attention, too much anger, irrational thoughts) behind her depression. Once you are able communicate and cooperate well with this part of you, you and she can work out a plan together to improve your quality of life.

The three examples described above explain why integration is an important process in the journey towards recovery. These examples also show how a traumatized person can achieve integration and recovery.

You can integrate your experiences only when you stay within the 'window of tolerance'

'Window of tolerance' refers to an optimal arousal level in which a person is functioning well and can effectively process his/her experiences. When a person is within his/her window of tolerance, he/she is more likely to be able to reflect. Signs of staying within the window of tolerance also include having empathy, thinking rationally, interacting with other people properly and being emotionally stable.

A traumatic or very stressful experience can push a person out of his/her window of tolerance. As a result, the person can become either hyper-aroused or hypo-aroused.

If he/she is above the window of tolerance, his/her 'fight/flight' stress response system will be activated. Thus, he/she will feel unsafe, frightened, panicky, angry, anxious, etc. He/she will be emotionally unstable. During this time, he/she will be unable to process or integrate his/her experiences.

If he/she is below the window of tolerance, his/her 'freeze' stress response system will be activated. Thus, he/she will feel numb, become unresponsive or very depressed, have no energy, or even lose his/her consciousness. During this time, he/she is also unable to process or integrate his/her experiences.

It is important for you to learn how to stay within your window of tolerance. Strategies such as grounding techniques and mindful breathing can effectively help you return to the window of tolerance. It is always possible to expand your window of tolerance by providing yourself a safe place, practicing mindfulness, having more self-awareness and developing healthy social relationships.

Let's review some important concepts related to trauma recovery

1. You are not crazy – You are just responding to adverse experiences

Some people with mental health problems believe that they have gone crazy. However, a person's mental health is not affected just by biological factors (e.g., genetic influences, chemicals in the brain). Many scientific studies have shown that mental health is also highly related to one's life experiences, especially interpersonal experiences.

If you have developed mental health problems after certain adverse, stressful or unhappy experiences (no matter how minor or severe they are), it means that your body and mind are responding to the experiences. Don't blame yourself, your body, your brain or your genes. Every part of you is trying to help you survive, although sometimes some of your parts may use unhealthy strategies.

2. There are reasons behind your symptoms and behaviors

Symptoms and behaviors come with reasons for them. No matter what problems you have, the presenting problems usually have reasons behind them or have meanings. Here are some examples:

- A person hears harsh voices from an internal family member because the family member has certain unaddressed needs (e.g., the family member wants to remind him/her about something, the family member does not have enough sense of safety)
- A person has an addiction to something (e.g., video games, alcohol) probably because he/she wants to avoid something (e.g., pain or stress)
- A person overeats frequently because he/she feels empty or powerless (eating becomes the only controllable thing for him/her)
- A person often criticizes others because he/she has learned this communication pattern from his/her parents or because he/she is afraid of being neglected

Can you see the reasons or meanings behind your problems? Don't just try to solve the problems, you also need to address the needs behind the problems!

3. Many things are just 'learned'

Many behaviors and symptoms are just 'learned'. Here are some examples:

- A person 'learns to' fear dogs after being bitten by a big dog
- A person 'learns to' be chronically dissociated after he/she realizes that dissociation can enable him/her to temporarily stay away from the overwhelming pain
- A person 'learns to' be phobic of his/her emotions and other internal parts (e.g., internal family members) because he/she is phobic of the painful memories that these parts hold
- A person does not have healthy boundaries with his/her friends because he/she did not learn them from his/her parents (i.e., he/she 'learns to' have arbitrary and unstable boundaries)

You can see that many things are just 'learned'. Although it takes time and requires hard work, you can always replace unhealthy behaviors by learning new behaviors!

As we all know, recovery looks difficult.

Please don't forget that the human brain is more plastic than we imagined, and can heal itself.

4. You are in charge

While you can't control or change what happened in the past, now that you have grown up, you have become more capable of protecting yourself. You can make a change now!

You are the one who can look for solutions for your problems

You are the one who can talk to your teammates inside

You are the one who can learn new things together with your teammates

You are the one who can develop teamwork with your body and mind

Therapists, social workers, psychiatrists, supportive friends or medications may help you a lot. However, no one and nothing can help you recover and integrate without hard work by you

Therapists or friends may be good supports and facilitators for you to communicate and work with your body and mind, but you are still in charge in your own recovery journey

Don't forget to co-lead your life with every part of you!!

All the best!!

Assignment 8.1

Can you recognize some of the reasons or meanings behind your existing symptoms/problems? You may do this by self-understanding, consulting your internal teammates or discussing with your therapist, if you have one. Please select a few symptoms/problems that you currently have, and then try to write down some possible reasons or meanings behind each symptom/problem.

Assignment 8.2

No matter whether they have a dissociative disorder or not, everyone needs to acknowledge, respect, thank and accept the inner parts of self. Have you ever tried self-talk? Please try to write a brief letter to yourself (including your known or not-yet-known inner parts) to share your thoughts with them. You may show your respect and gratitude to them, talk about your wishes, propose some follow-up communication and collaboration with them, tell them what you have learned recently, or even ask some questions.

Question 1: Does the content in this chapter relate to your experience?
1 = Strongly disagree; 10 = Strongly agree

Question 2: Have you learned this content before?
1 = Strongly disagree; 10 = Strongly agree

Chapter 9: Common Questions About Trauma And Dissociation

This chapter aims to:

1. Answer some frequently asked questions about trauma and dissociation
2. Provide some practical advice for readers to reduce confusion

Question 1: How could I confirm if I have PTSD, BPD, and/or DID, etc?

Answer 1: If you want to confirm whether you have certain mental disorders, you basically need to consult a qualified psychiatrist or clinical psychologist. During the assessment, you will be interviewed clinically. Some assessment tools (e.g., questionnaires) may be used too. You may also consult more than one psychiatrist or clinical psychologist.

Question 2: I have some hazy memories of abuse by someone. Did they really happen?

Answer 2: Until now, there is no scientific method to determine whether certain memories are 'real' or not. Many factors could affect the validity of our memories. A wise way to handle hazy memories is to be open-minded. No need to force yourself to remember or forget anything. Whether or not the trauma really happened in the past, the way to recover from post-traumatic and dissociative symptoms is the same – remain safe, learn healthy coping skills, accept each part of you, be a teammate with yourself, and integrate your biopsychosocial experiences gradually. During the process of recovery, you may have more clues that enable you to know more about yourself.

Question 3: Can I recover from trauma and dissociation by simply having medication treatments?

Answer 3: In some cases, medications can be very helpful in managing some presenting symptoms (e.g., depression, insomnia). Some medications may have small positive impacts on certain post-traumatic symptoms. However, until now, there is no evidence that medications can help a person process and integrate his/her trauma or dissociated parts of the personality. It is also important to be aware of the potential side effects of medications. In the literature, it has been reported that some medications may worsen certain dissociative symptoms. Different dissociated personality states of the same person may respond to medications differently too. Psychosocial interventions (e.g., psychotherapy) are primary treatments for post-traumatic mental disorders.

Question 4: Do I have multiple 'personalities'?

Answer 4: As mentioned in the previous chapter, each person has a lot of different parts, but these parts are the parts of a single personality system. A person is in fact the sum of all his/her parts. Thus, scholars in the field believe that no one has multiple 'personalities'. In patients with DID, some parts may feel like they are totally individual persons. No matter what you believe, it is important to work as a mutually-supportive team.

Question 5: What does 'internal family members' (or internal teammates) mean?

Answer 5: 'Internal family members' is not an academic term. Both 'internal family members' and 'internal teammates' refer to the internal parts of a person. We use these two terms (same meaning) in order to emphasize that internal parts are very close to us and that we need to communicate and cooperate with these internal parts.

Question 6: How is DID different from schizophrenia?

Answer 6: DID and schizophrenia are two mental disorders in two different diagnostic categories. In DSM-5, DID is in the category of 'Dissociative Disorders' while schizophrenia is in the category of 'Schizophrenia Spectrum And Other Psychotic Disorders'. Historically, it was generally believed that DID is trauma-related and schizophrenia is biologically related, and that DID requires psychotherapy and schizophrenia requires medication treatments. However, studies in recent years showed that the situation is not that simple. For example, childhood trauma in patients with schizophrenia is also fairly common; the clinical presentations of DID and schizophrenia have overlapped (e.g., both may have auditory hallucinations); and, patients with schizophrenia also need psychological and social care.

Two major differences between DID and schizophrenia are that: (1) psychological amnesia and (2) identity alteration are features of DID but not of schizophrenia. Besides those differences, impairment of reality testing may occur in people with DID but usually does not last long, whereas impairment of reality testing is a feature of psychosis (schizophrenia is regarded as a psychotic disorder). Impairment of reality testing means that a person is unable to distinguish subjective experiences from the external world (e.g., a person with impaired reality testing believes that other persons can also hear the content of his/her auditory hallucinations, or – as a result of delusional thinking – firmly believes that someone in outside reality is really going to hurt him/her). Even this criterion is not that simple, however, because trauma survivors are commonly afraid that others will hurt them in the future, just as they have in the past.

People with schizophrenia often have a severe thought disorder, which is rare in DID, or, if it occurs, is short in duration. People with schizophrenia may have very disorganized thought processes, and very bizarre delusional beliefs, and may use words in a very odd way. These features are not seen in DID.

Question 7: Is it possible for patients with DID to realize that they have other dissociated personality states (also known as identity states)?

Answer 7: Yes, it is possible. Patients with DID may have different levels of amnesia and co-consciousness, ranging from not knowing each other to having excellent internal communication.

Question 8: Is it true that patients with DID always have amnesia?

Answer 8: Yes. In DSM-5, psychological amnesia is one of the diagnostic criteria for DID. However, there are different forms of psychological amnesia, such as amnesia for some personal information, amnesia for certain past experiences, memory gaps in daily life and loss of well-learned skills or knowledge. If a person does not have obvious psychological amnesia but still suffers from significant dissociative symptoms, a diagnosis of OSDD may be considered.

Question 9: What can I do if I feel that my psychiatrist does not understand my condition?

Answer 9: It can be a very difficult time if your psychiatrist does not understand you. First of all, you need to try your best to communicate with your psychiatrist. If that does not work, there are still several possible solutions for you to consider. You may seek help from your social worker (or a reliable friend), ask him/her to go to consultation with you, and see if he/she can improve your communication with your psychiatrist. You may also consider consulting another psychiatrist. It is important to find a psychiatrist who is experienced in treating your condition (e.g., if you have a dissociative disorder, try to find a psychiatrist who has experience in treating patients with dissociative disorders, or at least a psychiatrist who is willing to learn about dissociative disorders).

However, it is sometimes really hard to find a suitable psychiatrist in your community. Therefore, some people even consider traveling a long way for treatment, although the cost is high. Even if a suitable psychiatrist is not available, there are patients who can still recover from trauma and dissociation. For example, they stay away trauma and stress, they have good social support, and they work hard to learn self-help skills and achieve internal harmony and internal cooperation.

Question 10: Should I tell other people about my trauma and dissociation?

Answer 10: It really depends. Having a person who understands you is important and helpful. However, there are risks. For instance, the person may not understand, may not believe in what you say, may criticize you, may use this to attack you, or may tell this to others even without your permission. It is necessary to think carefully before you make the decision.

Question 11: What is the difference between 'integration' and 'fusion'?

Answer 11: Integration of the personality refers to a process in which a person acknowledges, accepts, communicates and cooperates with the internal parts. In the context of DID, 'fusion' refers to the situation in which two or more dissociated personality states 'experience themselves as joining together with a complete loss of subjective separateness', according to the guidelines of the ISSTD in 2011. Fusion involves two personality states joining together at a particular time, whereas integration is a gradual process. Integration is the goal of recovery from trauma. Some people with DID decide to have full integration while others do not (i.e., they decide to live as a well-functioning team). It is possible to reach integration without fusion if the personality states just gradually de-differentiate and blend together over time.

Question 12: Is everything just my imagination or fantasy?

Answer 12: With normal imagination or fantasy, you should be able to control your experience and stop it whenever you want. If the things you imagine lead to significant distress or impairment, that should alert you that something is wrong and needs to be addressed. Dissociation is created by the mind, but this does not mean it is 'made up' and can be switched off. The dissociative reactions were there to help you survive in childhood. Usually, concerns that the dissociative reactions are just 'made up' are a way of avoiding the other team members.

Question 13: How can I find a therapist who is experienced in treating trauma and dissociation?

Answer 13: This question is difficult to answer in many countries and regions. In some places, a therapist for DID is hard to find. You may talk to your social worker or doctor and see if he/she can make a referral. You may also try to go to the Internet and search for a therapist who has talked about trauma and dissociation or published papers on related topics.

Question 14: Is it possible to heal without receiving treatment?

Answer 14: Yes, it is possible. If you can stay away from trauma and stress, have good social support and work hard on integration, your chance of recovery will definitely increase. There are people who recover from trauma and dissociation even without formal treatment. Yet, for many people, treatment is needed.

Assignment 9.1

This chapter tries to answer some common questions. Has it answered some questions you have had and reduced your confusion? Try to summarize what you have learned or write down your reflections in some sentences.

Assignment 9.2

Although there may be many bad things in our lives, there must be some good things as well. Can you identify some good things in your current life?

Question 1: Does the content in this chapter relate to your experience?
1 = Strongly disagree; 10 = Strongly agree

Question 2: Have you learned this content before?
1 = Strongly disagree; 10 = Strongly agree

Chapter 10: Coping With Dissociative Reactions

This chapter aims to:

1. Enable readers to better understand dissociative reactions
2. Discuss some principles and strategies for coping with dissociative reactions

Dissociative reactions are protective in nature. Dissociative reactions are creative and adaptive strategies that the mind uses for surviving trauma and stress, allowing the victim to continue to manage daily life (e.g., learn in class, socially engage with friends) despite having overwhelming experiences. Having said that, troubles resulting from dissociative reactions can be very real. Recurrent dissociative reactions can seriously interfere with a person's life. Therefore, treatment is important, especially specialized psychotherapy. In addition, knowing how to cope with dissociative reactions in daily life will be very helpful. This chapter discusses some principles and strategies for coping with dissociative reactions.

Before discussing the principles and strategies, you need to know that the presentations of dissociative reactions can be diverse.

Dr. Marlene Steinberg, author of the book *The Stranger in the Mirror: Dissociation – The Hidden Epidemic*, suggested that there are five core dissociative symptoms [1]:

1. Amnesia
2. Depersonalization
3. Derealization
4. Identity confusion
5. Identity alteration

On the other hand, Dr. Paul F. Dell, developer of the assessment tool The Multidimensional Inventory of Dissociation (MID), proposed that there are 23 different dissociative symptoms [2]:

1. General dissociative symptoms
    a. General memory problems

---

1 Steinberg, M., & Schnall, M. (2000). *The stranger in the mirror: Dissociation—The hidden epidemic*. New York: HarperCollins.

2 Dell, P. F. (2009). The phenomena of pathological dissociation. In P. F. Dell & J. A. O'Neil (Eds.), *Dissociation and the dissociative disorders: DSM-V and beyond (pp. 228-233)*. New York: Routledge.

   b. Depersonalization
   c. Derealization
   d. Post-traumatic flashbacks
   e. Somatoform symptoms
   f. Trance states (e.g., absence-like staring and unresponsiveness)

2. Intrusions of another self-state (personality state) – partial dissociation
   a. Hearing child voices
   b. Hearing or feeling internal struggles
   c. Hearing harsh or persecutory voices
   d. Speech insertion (e.g., speak out something as if it does not come from you)
   e. Thought insertion or withdrawal
   f. Made or intrusive feelings and emotions
   g. Made or intrusive impulses
   h. Made or intrusive actions
   i. Temporary loss of well-rehearsed knowledge or skills
   j. Self-alteration
   k. Self-puzzlement (e.g., you are confused about who you are and why you do or feel something)

3. Full dissociation – Amnesia
   a. Time loss
   b. 'Coming to' (e.g., you suddenly realize that you are doing something in a situation, but you cannot remember what happened even 10 seconds ago)
   c. Fugues (e.g., you suddenly 'wake up' in a place, but you do not remember how/when/why you come to this place)
   d. Being told of disremembered actions
   e. Finding objects among your possessions
   f. Finding evidence of one's recent actions

While these dissociative symptoms are common in persons with a dissociative disorder, some of them (e.g., depersonalization, derealization, flashbacks, somatoform symptoms) also occur in persons with other mental disorders, such as PTSD, BPD and panic disorder.

Some important principles in coping with dissociative reactions are as follows:

1. You need to acknowledge the fact that there are reasons behind the dissociative reactions. Dissociative reactions do not come without reasons. To fully cure pathological dissociation, you will need to find out the reasons behind it and address the underlying

problems. Usually, your inner parts know much more than you know. It is often helpful to consult them humbly.

2. You need to remain safe and stay in the present moment. When dissociative reactions occur, it is very likely that you do not feel safe enough, that you are affected by an intrusion from the past, or that some parts of you are mired in the past. If you can bring yourself (and your internal teammates) back to the here and now, you can have a sense of safety – dissociative reactions will no longer be necessary when you are safe enough.

3. You need to work hard on integration – accept your inner parts, respect them, talk to them, consult them humbly, and work with them as a team. Very often, dissociative symptoms can be resolved by resolving the internal conflicts or the problems facing some parts of you. Promoting internal harmony (internal communication, internal cooperation) is a crucial way to reduce dissociative symptoms.

Situation 1: I cannot recall the memory of some important life events. What can I do?

The memory may be held by other parts of you, or the memory may be too overwhelming for you. Do not force yourself to recall the memory. You need to address the problems (if any) that interfere with your current daily life first. You need to stay away from trauma and stress and stabilize your condition (reduce the symptoms). If you want to recall the memory, you first need to ensure that you are fully ready to face and process the dissociated memory.

Situation 2: I feel like there are serious internal conflicts inside my mind – sometimes I want to do this, sometimes I want to do that, and sometimes I even have strange feelings, emotions or impulses. What can I do?

You need to acknowledge the fact that everyone has a lot of different parts – it is very normal that some parts of you want to do this while other parts of you want to do that. To settle internal conflicts, you may try self-talk – talk to yourself and your internal teammates, understand the needs of the other parts of you, and come to a compromise that all parts of you can accept. In order to know why you have some strange feelings, emotions or impulses, you may also try to consult your inner parts humbly – they may get back to you by sending you some visuals, voices, thoughts, or even dreams. Whether or not you have a dissociative disorder, internal communication and cooperation are the primary solutions to internal conflicts.

Situation 3: When I get triggered, I always have some painful memories that come back to me in a flood. What can I do?

You may have dissociative flashbacks. Even if you do not have them, it is possible that some parts of you have dissociative flashbacks. You can use the skills you have learned (e.g., grounding techniques) to cope with flashbacks. You also need to help your inner parts to cope with flashbacks – bring them back to the present moment, hold them warmly, and reassure them that it is safe now.

Situation 4: I feel like I have a child inside my mind, and she keeps crying. What can I do?

A child cries because there are some unaddressed needs (e.g., feeling hungry, unsafe or painful). Similarly, a child inside keeps crying because of some unaddressed needs. Just like any other part of you, she is a part of you too. You cannot ignore her. It may be difficult to do so, but you need to take care of her – hold her, talk to her, make her feel safe, understand her, and address her needs. She was there for some purpose in the past, but the situation has changed (e.g., the stressor is no longer here). Now you can help her transfer her roles, functions and duties – for example, is there anything she can help with now?

Situation 5: I hear some voices that often argue inside or comment on me harshly. What can I do?

You need to know if the voices are a kind of flashback (i.e., repeating what someone said in the past). If the voices come from a dissociated part of you, it is likely that antipsychotic medications could not fully treat the voices. You may have a phobia of these voices, but you need to understand them in order to manage them. Are they responsive? Are they representing some parts of you? Although they may look unfriendly, it is likely that they are sending you some messages (e.g., reminding you to do or not to do something, drawing your attention to some unaddressed needs). If the voices are responsive (i.e., they respond to you in a logical way), try to talk to them and build a good relationship with them. If they are trapped in the past, tell them that the past is gone and that you are safe now. You can also give them some time to talk every day and tell them when you cannot talk to them. Even it is an angry part, it is in fact a teammate of yours. Sincere communication is a wise way to transform an enemy into a friend.

Situation 6: I often have medically unexplained physical symptoms (e.g., sudden loss of consciousness, temporary loss of voice,

temporary inability to use some parts of the body, pain). The doctor does not know why these symptoms occur. What can I do?

Try to identify if there is any stressor or trigger for the somatoform symptoms (e.g., what happened before you started to have the symptom?). You can also consult your inner parts humbly – some parts of you may know something you do not know. Besides, it is also possible that the suffering of some inner parts results in the somatoform symptoms. Take good care of your inner parts, then the symptoms may be resolved.

Situation 7: I usually suffer from depersonalization/derealization – it's like I am a robot, I cannot feel anything, sometimes I feel unreal, and sometimes other people/things look strange too. What can I do?

Try to identify if there is any stressor or trigger for the depersonalization/derealization symptoms. If there are any, you may consider staying away from them. Grounding techniques and practicing mindful breathing can help you come back to the present moment. Sometimes depersonalization/derealization may be the result of flashbacks. Sometimes, you (or some part of you) learned to depersonalize in order to avoid some overwhelming feelings or emotions. Sometimes, you (or some part of you) does not feel safe enough, and therefore you avoid having any feelings. In the context of being traumatized, symptoms always come with reasons. Thus, you need to find out the reasons behind depersonalization/derealization and tackle the underlying problems. You also need to create a sense of safety for yourself and your internal teammates.

Situation 8: I cannot see or talk to my internal members. There is no way to start internal communication. What can I do?

Everyone has different parts. No matter whether you have a dissociative disorder or not, you can try self-talk – yes, talk to yourself. You can do it by writing a journal or reflection logs, speaking to yourself directly (and of course gently and respectfully), or even initiating a meeting inside your mind. Some people can have wonderful internal meetings using their imaginations. If there is evidence that you have some dissociated personality states (e.g., you have recurrent memory gaps, your friend tells you that you have obvious personality switching, or you find things that do not belong to you) but you cannot communicate with them, you may feel very confused and frustrated. There are some possible reasons that you cannot communicate with them. For instance, you are avoiding them, you do not show enough respect to them, they are afraid of you, they do not feel safe enough, they do not trust you, or they do not even know who you are. Although it is not easy, it is important for you to make efforts to start communication with them. In the beginning, you may try to write a journal or write some letters to them. Make them feel safe and let them know what is going on. Let them know you welcome them and they can talk to you. Even if there are memory barriers and you cannot talk to your internal teammates, you need to figure out a way to communicate with them. For instance, it is possible to have asynchronous communication (not real-time communication) with your dissociated personality states through writing letters, sending messages or other means.

Situation 9: I have time loss (memory gaps) frequently. What can I do?

Writing in your journal regularly can be a helpful way to cope with dissociative amnesia. If you have recurrent dissociative amnesia, it is likely that you have certain dissociated parts – no matter whether they are memory fragments, emotional parts, or fully developed dissociated personality states. You can try to talk to them. You need to start internal communication and cooperation with them. You need to work together with them and find out some possible solutions. For example, can you share some time with them so that they do not need to 'steal' your time? Can they share their memories with you? Is it possible for you to do things together (e.g., co-hosting or co-fronting)? Once you can overcome the internal conflicts and share time and memory with your internal teammates, dissociative amnesia can be reduced.

Situation 10: Some parts of me do not trust my therapist. What can I do?

While the therapist needs to assess the client, the client (including his/her internal parts) also assesses the therapist. It is understandable. The client needs to know whether the therapist is trustworthy and whether it is safe to tell the therapist some personal or secret things. Try to discuss this with your internal teammates and see if you can work towards a consensus regarding your treatment with the therapist. However, please remember that it sometimes takes time to know if a therapist is suitable for you. You also need to see if the therapist is willing to acknowledge and respect other parts of you.

Situation 11: Some parts of me often do inappropriate things (e.g., spend too much money, buy too many things, refuse to work). What can I do?

Internal conflicts can greatly affect your life. Unfortunately, no medications can treat such internal conflicts. No matter whether you have a dissociative disorder or not, you need to take care of your internal teammates, talk to them, understand them, and cooperate with them. It is just like conflicts in a friend group or in a team, some members may do 'inappropriate' things. Sometimes you need to educate or help your members. Sometimes you need to set rules and discipline your members. Sometimes you need to reach a compromise with them. You must find a way to achieve a consensus and develop teamwork. You need to be patient. Usually it is not easy. However, sincere and rational communication can make things work.

Situation 12: Some parts of me are very depressed. What can I do?

After long-lasting trauma and stress, it is understandable to be depressed, isn't it? There are enough reasons for you (or some parts of you) to be sad. However, if some parts of you have chronic depression, you may be able to help them. It should be noted that, in cases of DID, it is possible for different personality states to have different mental health problems – for example, one part has depression, one part has PTSD for Event A, while another part has PTSD for Event B. You need to help your internal teammates handle their problems. They need your support and care. A depressed part may be holding some painful memories, may be suppressing some 'dangerous' emotions (e.g., anger), or may not even know how to be happy. The depression of this part may make you depressed too. Therefore, take good care of your internal teammates, give a hand to them!

Situation 13: Some parts of me are very aggressive and uncooperative. What can I do?

There must be some reasons behind this problem. Typically speaking, your inner parts are here to serve certain purposes, even though the purposes are not always clear. Imagine a cat that has been hurt before, what behaviors may it have? The cat may shrink back, may be angry (so that it can look strong to protect itself), and may no longer trust people (so that it can avoid being hurt again). It is also possible that these parts form because you have internalized the characteristics (e.g., behaviors) of some people you met in your life (e.g., someone who hurt you before). If you have some parts that are aggressive or uncooperative, you need to understand them, acknowledge their roles as protectors, and realize that they may also be suffering. It is very likely that these parts are protecting you in some way, even in an unimaginable way, and even if they do not believe that they mean to help you.

Situation 14: Some parts of me (e.g., the host personality, or the little one) disappear. What's going on?

As long as a part of the personality forms, it never truly disappears. It may hide, it may be unavailable, it may be suppressed, or it may fuse together with some other parts. Even in the context of DID, a dissociated personality state will not truly 'die', 'disappear' or be eliminated. A part may 'disappear' willingly or unwillingly. You need to try to understand the reasons behind this. If it is really the choice of that part, you may need to respect the decision. Try to maintain communication (no matter if they are here to listen or not – it is always possible for them to receive your messages even if they do not appear to be here), give a hand to your internal teammates, and see what they need.

Situation 15: Some parts of me want to hurt or kill other inner parts. What can I do?

A part that has formed will never truly get killed or eliminated. Yet, of course, your internal teammates may get hurt. Hence, you need to resolve the conflicts inside. To take care of your teammates, sometimes you need to be a good babysitter, sometimes you need to be a good teacher and information provider, sometimes you need to be a good communication facilitator, sometimes you need to be a good democratic leader, and sometimes you need to be a good conflict mediator. Listen to different parties, understand their needs, investigate why they have conflicts, make rational judgements, promote teamwork, propose alternatives, and facilitate consensus. Although it is hard, try your best to be just – every part in the team is equal. Some people like having regular meetings inside or even doing things together (e.g., eating) in the inner world. This can effectively promote cooperation and mutual aid among your internal teammates. You may want to try to organize your own inner group activities too!

Situation 16: There is evidence that suggests that I may have a new internal teammate. What can I do?

Many people whose personality dissociates discover new inner parts even after many years. Some parts hid, and therefore you did not know them in the past. It is also possible that some parts form as you have new experiences in your life. No worries. If you are not yet sure if there is a new part, just be open-minded, create a warm and safe inner world and welcome every possibility. If you have already found the new part, you may talk to him/her, understand him/her and try to be friends with him/her – just like you are meeting a new person in your life. Of course, your new friend may resist to a certain degree in the beginning. Try to make him/her feel safe and let him/her become a member in your team/ group.

Situation 17: After some traumatic or stressful events, the inner world gets broken, and the little ones inside my mind are frightened. What can I do?

An inner world is the world that you – intentionally or unintentionally – create through imagery inside your mind. Ideally, the inner world is a safe place in which you can communicate and cooperate with your internal teammates. You can have a big, warm, mutually-supportive family/team/group/community in your inner world. Sometimes, your inner world may have interactions with your experience in the external world. For example, if you encounter some stressful situations, there may be some effects on your inner world too. However, you should remember that you are in charge in your inner world. If it gets broken, you can fix it, or even make it be a more beautiful place – use some imagination! Make good use of your inner world to promote internal harmony and internal cooperation. Don't forget to take care of your child parts too.

Situation 18: Some parts of me often occupy the body. This results in recurrent memory gaps and distressful identity alteration (personality switching). What can I do?

You need to talk to your internal teammates, see what they expect and what you can do for them; try to come to a compromise that all parts of you can accept. You need to tell them when they can and cannot come out (i.e., use the body) – for example, you may want to give your little teammates some time to play games or toys at night, while you do not allow them to come out when you are on duty. In a team/group, it is unavoidable that there are different opinions sometimes. Of course, you may want to force your teammates to do or not to do something or you may also want to suppress them, but you should know that 'the greater the force, the greater the reaction force'. It is more appropriate to resolve conflicts through communication and collaboration.

Assignment 10.1

If there is a place in which you can feel very very safe and very very warm, what would this place be? Based on your previous experience or imagination, can you describe a place where you would like to get a good rest?

Assignment 10.2

No matter whether you have a dissociative disorder or not, you need to look after your body and mind – your internal teammates. Are there any positive things (e.g., encouragement, gratitude, or useful information) that your internal teammates want to tell you? Try to listen to these positive things – you may do it by imagination, role-playing or really listening to your mind. What good things do you get?

Question 1: Does the content in this chapter relate to your experience?
1 = Strongly disagree; 10 = Strongly agree

Question 2: Have you learned this content before?
1 = Strongly disagree; 10 = Strongly agree

Chapter 11: Interpersonal Issues In Trauma Recovery

This chapter aims to:

1. Discuss internal relationship issues with internal team members.
2. Discuss relationship issues with outside people during trauma recovery.

How to get along with your team members

We have discussed relationships with inside team members throughout this book. In this chapter we will provide some reminders and some additional suggestions. While we focus on the context of DID in this part, persons whose personality dissociates should also learn how to handle relationship issues with their internal team members even if they do not meet the diagnostic criteria for DID.

First, it is important for the part out front – often called *the host personality* in the DID literature – to realize that he or she is not 'the person.' The host personality is just one part. The job of the host personality is to be the host personality – that is, be in control of the body most of the time, go to school, be a parent, go to work, and to function in the outside world. In order to do this job, the host personality, or out front part, cannot know and feel all the emotions, memories and conflicts, otherwise he or she would be flooded, overwhelmed, and unable to function. The whole purpose of DID is to split the trauma up into pieces so that no one part holds everything, and so the out front part can function.

DID is a great survival strategy during childhood while the trauma is still going on. In adulthood, when the trauma has stopped, however, it can cause more problems than it solves; switching, amnesia, conflicts, unhealthy behavior, and general chaos and disorganization on both the outside and the inside. That is why some therapy work and reorganization is required.

A first step is for the out front person to stop thinking, feeling and acting like he or she is the real person, and the other parts are just parts. Similarly, it is not true that the body is the out front person's body. All parts are parts of the whole and all share ownership of the body. This can be a difficult concept early in recovery when some parts still believe that they have their own separate physical bodies. The out front person needs to take the lead on understanding, accepting and telling the others that everyone is in this together.

Also, the out front person needs to let go of the wish to get rid of the other parts. This only causes resentment, anger, suicidal ideation, feeling unloved and unaccepted, and counter-hostility towards the out front person. Is it surprising that if the out front person wants to get rid of the other parts, the other parts respond by wanting to kill the out front person? Often, the suicidal parts do not understand that if they kill the host personality, everyone dies, including them. Other times, the parts realize that they will die too, but they don't care.

A key point to grasp is that all parts are part of the survival system. This includes angry, hostile, suicidal and self-punishing parts. The strategies they use for survival, such as cutting, may be self-destructive and unhealthy, and they may need to stop, but this is not just 'bad behavior' for no reason. The purpose of the behavior needs to be understood and healthy coping strategies need to be learned, so that the unhealthy strategies are no longer required. Trying to take away the unhealthy behaviors without replacing them with healthy coping strategies may not work. The parts doing the cutting or other unhealthy behaviors will feel like their power, control and reason for existing are being taken away from them.

The self-destructive parts need to be thanked for trying to help. The idea is not to get rid of them. They should be accepted as valuable team members. Their basic jobs of protecting, holding anger, coming out when there is a threat, and so on, do not need to change. These are valuable tools in the overall survival plan. They do need some adjustment, however. For specific strategies, exercises and tasks to get along better with your team members, look back at the previous chapters in this book. These strategies include:

- Writing letters to the parts
- Holding internal team meetings
- Talking to the parts inside
- Letting the parts have time in therapy sessions
- Assigning times for parts to come out and do healthy activities
- Creating safe places inside that are pleasant
- Making deals with parts
- Journaling back and forth with parts
- Working on co-consciousness
- Finding alternative jobs and activities for parts

- Including parts in fun activities

All of these tasks can be done when you start to develop internal communication and cooperation. Many of the tasks are suitable as 'inner child work' even if there are no structured, separate parts. Everyone has an inner child in the sense of unresolved feelings from childhood. Even when the inner child is just a metaphor, many of these exercises can be useful. They can be done as if there is a separate inner child, even when this is only a metaphor.

Much of the recovery work in DID is just basic human being work – it isn't all about working with dissociated parts. It's important to try to find a balance between working as a whole person and working with the parts. It is possible to be out of balance in either direction – ignoring the parts too much, or spending too much time absorbed in the inner world and all the interactions of the parts. Like everything in recovery, it is a matter of balance. Sometimes the emphasis will need to be on parts work for a while, but at other times it is important to focus on current day problems, the outside world and a whole person perspective.

You will never get it right all the time, and there is no formula for exactly how much to focus on the parts. You can be certain that you will get it wrong sometimes. That's just part of recovery. Don't beat yourself up. Just correct the imbalance and get back to work.

How to get along with outside people

Getting along with other people is an endless, big job for everyone. Unfortunately, there are quite a few toxic people on the planet. Many of our supposed role models, like political leaders, corporate executives, academics, and mental health professionals are not very good role models. They provide examples of ugly, hostile, exploitive behavior towards others, including sexism, racism, verbal abuse, putting other people down, lying, exploiting other people for personal gain, and a long list of other unhealthy behaviors.

It may not be possible to have a healthy relationship with certain individuals. Part of the work of recovery is making new, healthy friends, and letting go of old, unhealthy friends. This can be a painful, lonely task when new relationships have not been built yet. For example, when someone is early in recovery from alcohol abuse, it may be necessary to stop seeing the old drinking buddies, and stop going to bars and social events where there is a lot of drinking.

When a trauma survivor has been in the rescuer role a lot, it can likewise be painful to realize that many of your friends don't want to see you unless you are taking care of them all the time, and ignoring your own needs.

Now, it is time to start taking care of your inside team members more, and taking care of outside people less.

Often, the survivor feels like spending time taking care of 'number 1' (oneself) is selfish. If you are a parent, taking care of yourself is actually the best thing you can do as a parent. Taking time out for number 1 is part of making yourself the best, healthiest parent possible. Children and spouses may not like the change, but really it is in their best interests long-term, even if they can't see that right now. Part of the work of recovery is letting go of guilt about stepping out of the caretaker role.

Another issue that comes up frequently is how much to tell other people about both your trauma and your dissociation. Again, it is possible to error in both directions. If you tell too many people too many details too fast, you can drive people away. This isn't proof that you are unlovable. Cancer patients often experience the same thing – many of their 'friends' can't cope with the cancer and disappear. This is when you learn who your real friends are. It's a painful process, but you end up with a smaller collection of true friends who you can focus on.

A good goodbye thought is, "See you. Wouldn't want to be you."

You don't have to say this out loud, but it is a good thought that can help make it be about the other person, not about you.

Generally, overall, it is better to err on the side of not telling too much too fast. There is no need to tell your trauma story to the checkout person at the supermarket, or all the details about your team members. Sometimes there is no need to tell anyone except your therapist. Usually, though, there are a few close friends, supports, relatives, partners or other people who want to know what is going on, and who can handle the information. Even for a spouse or partner, though, it is not necessary to tell all the details. Again, there is no formula or one size fits all.

Some spouses are so toxic and abusive that separation and divorce are necessary. This can be a very difficult process emotionally, financially and in many ways. It activates the problem of attachment to the perpetrator very intensely. Other relationships are definitely sound and healthy, and there is no need to even think about divorce. Many relationships are somewhere in the middle and there is no easy answer. Not uncommonly, as one person works hard on recovery, makes changes, and grows, the other partner stays stuck and cannot adjust to the changes. Gradually, the two people grow apart. The eventual separation may be mutually agreed upon and done in a healthy way, or the partner left behind may become accusatory, blaming and angry, or may take the victim role. All those things are their problem, not yours.

The same problem can occur with parents who were abusive in childhood.

Some parents are so toxic in the present that they need to be 'divorced.' Some were never the perpetrators and are not a problem in the present. Others – not many – were severe perpetrators in the past but have admitted what they did, apologized, made real changes, and are now good supports. Others are somewhere in the middle – not so toxic that they need to be cut off, but needing some boundaries and limits on the amount of contact and interaction.

Some parents are not outright abusive, just enmeshed and co-dependent. When you become healthier and start getting your own life, they may feel abandoned and may react with accusations, crises in which they need you to come in as the rescuer, or other behaviors that can cause a lot of guilt. Your task is to stand strong, take care of yourself, and be compassionate, but not get sucked back in. This is easy for the therapist to say, but not so easy for you to do.

Overall, the goal for every parent should be for the children to grow up, become independent and have productive, healthy lives. When you work on this, you are not being a bad child. You are being a good child and are making your parents look like successful parents, even if they don't see that.

When you have to start focusing on difficulties in present-day relationships, that is good news. It means you are no longer trapped in the past. Welcome to the human race! It isn't always fun, but it is progress.

A common problem area in intimate relationships is sex. For people with PTSD from childhood sexual abuse, this can be a very big problem. There are therapists who specialize in 'sex therapy' and it might be helpful to consult one as a couple. This would be added onto your individual therapy, and would not replace it. Sometimes such a therapy will focus on relationship problems, and sometimes it will involve desensitization exercises.

For example, if full intercourse is too triggering, you can start by agreeing to just hold hands, but not go any further. When you are comfortable with this, you can progress to stroking arms or hands, then kissing, then step-by-step adding on more sexual behaviors at a pace you can tolerate.

Another common problem in intimate relationships is that the partner blames all the relationship problems on the trauma survivor, and won't admit to being part of the problem himself or herself. Couple therapy may be worth trying in that situation. Some partners can take responsibility for their behaviors, but some just won't. In that case, you have to balance the positive aspects of the relationship against the negatives, and decide how long to stay in the relationship. Making a commitment to yourself to stay in the relationship till all the children are out of high school can be good for some people. For others, the same decision is based on denial, rationalization and procrastination. Usually, a mixture of all these factors is in play, and there is no clear-cut path to take. Again, welcome to the human race.

Sometimes it is necessary to have a moratorium on full sexual intercourse while you are working on the PTSD. It can be helpful to make sure all the child parts are asleep inside before any sexual activity starts. Sometimes there is a more sexual part who can handle normal sexual activity with the partner. This can be fine. It doesn't have to be the host personality. The task then is to gradually work on co-consciousness at a tolerable pace. Perhaps you can figure out ways to meet your partner's needs without having to engage in sexual intercourse. An unhealthy solution is for the host personality to send out traumatized alters to handle the sex, resulting in them feeling re-traumatized, used, and of no value for anything else.

As for most complicated relationship problems, there is often no easy solution, no matter what the problem. Family therapy can be helpful if children or other family members are involved or being affected by what's going on with the adults. For children, overall, the less they are told about your trauma and dissociation, the better. Certainly, you shouldn't explain trauma and dissociation to children under 10. Some early or mid-teenagers may be able to handle some information, but others would be overwhelmed by it.

Sometimes, children already know parts even before the diagnosis is made by a mental health professional. It may be useful to bring them into a therapy session to talk about dissociation, or it may not be necessary. Some children can handle more than others, at all ages. Just be careful not to put your children in the role of caretaker, parent for you, or best friend. These principles apply to everyone in your life. It's a balance between telling too much and telling too little. If you're unsure, or not ready, err on the side of telling too little until things become more clear.

For employers, generally, the less they know the better. Sometimes they need to be filled in for leave, disability or other reasons. It's probably better to say you have PTSD, anxiety or depression than to share a DID or OSDD diagnosis. That sets off fewer alarm bells in the outside system. Not telling all the details does not equal lying. It's your business, not theirs. Don't get pressured into telling more than you want to tell.

Strategies for dealing with problems and conflicts in relationships with outside people can include:

- Take a short time out before reacting
- Consult your therapist before taking any big steps
- Give yourself time to figure things out

- Use your grounding skills
- Try to figure out if you are reacting from the past
- Remember you don't owe anyone excessive self-sacrifice or caretaking
- Consider couple or family therapy
- Talk it over with someone you can trust
- Try reading self-help or relationship books, attending seminars or watching videos online
- Don't buy that you are always 100% of the problem
- Realize that you may have to let go of some people

Often, relationships on the inside mirror relationships on the outside, and vice versa. If you are disconnected from your internal team members, you may be disconnected from outside people as well. It is hard for others to love you if you don't love yourself. Remember to take care of the inside relationships. Often, the outside problems cannot be addressed or solved until the inside team is working together better. Be kind to yourself. Then others will be more likely to be kind to you.

Assignment 11.1

Write down a list of strategies you have used to work on relationships with your inside team members. Rate each one from 0 to 10 in terms of how helpful each one has been. Then write down a list of relationship strategies you haven't used, or haven't used enough. Make a plan for trying them out.

Assignment 11.2

Write down a list of strategies you have used to work on relationships with outside people. Rate each one from 0 to 10 in terms of how helpful each one has been. Then write down a list of relationship strategies you haven't used, or haven't used enough. Make a plan for trying them out.

Question 1: Does the content in this chapter relate to your experience?
1 = Strongly disagree; 10 = Strongly agree

Question 2: Have you learned this content before?
1 = Strongly disagree; 10 = Strongly agree

Chapter 12: Living Well During And After Trauma Recovery

This chapter aims to:

1. Discuss things readers can work on as part of their recovery in order to live well

A lot of trauma recovery work does not involve the trauma or the dissociation. It is just human being work. A list of things to work on in order to live well, besides the trauma work and the relationship work discussed in the previous chapter is:

- A healthy diet
- An exercise program
- A weight loss program if required
- Taking care of medical problems and needs
- Get enough sleep and enough quality sleep
- Getting more education or job training
- Finding a job that brings both money and personal satisfaction
- Having hobbies, interests and activities
- Scheduling a date night with your partner if you are a busy parent
- Travel and vacations if you can afford them
- Spending time in nature or at the beach
- Volunteering or doing community work
- Having one or more pets
- Taking care of finances including paying off debt
- Living in as healthy a neighborhood as possible
- Taking time out for yourself
- Making amends with people you have hurt
- Making an effort to reach out to others – this can be for many reasons
- Having an up to date will, insurance and other arrangements in place
- Working on your retirement planning – now not later
- Anything else you need or want – within reason

None of these things have to involve specific trauma or dissociation techniques. They are at least as important as the trauma work, in fact probably more important. This is true for both trauma clients and trauma therapists. It is important for the therapist to have a life outside trauma therapy. This prevents burnout and helps the therapist be more attuned and focused during therapy.

Overall, it is important to remember that you are a human being first, and a trauma survivor second. Taking care of all these normal human needs is just as important as your trauma work. You deserve to have a life. So go get one!

Assignment 12.1

Write down a list of your 'living well' tasks. Which ones have you taken care of, which ones have you worked on a little bit, and which ones have you ignored? Set some priorities, a time line and a sequence for working on these different tasks.

Question 1: Does the content in this chapter relate to your experience?
1 = Strongly disagree; 10 = Strongly agree

Question 2: Have you learned this content before?
1 = Strongly disagree; 10 = Strongly agree